Life *without* Limits

Life *without* Limits

THE DAVID PESCUD STORY

HELEN O'NEILL

BANTAM BOOKS

SYDNEY • AUCKLAND • TORONTO • NEW YORK • LONDON

LIFE WITHOUT LIMITS
A BANTAM BOOK

First published in Australia and New Zealand in 2003 by Bantam

National Library of Australia
Cataloguing-in-Publication entry:

O'Neill, H. (Helen).
Life without limits: the David Pescud story.

ISBN 1 86325 373 4.

1. Pescud, David. 2. Yacht racing – Australia. 3. Entrepreneurs – Australia – Biography. I. Title.

797.14092

Transworld Publishers,
a division of Random House Australia Pty Ltd
20 Alfred Street, Milsons Point, NSW 2061
http://www.randomhouse.com.au

Random House New Zealand Limited
18 Poland Road, Glenfield, Auckland

Transworld Publishers,
a division of The Random House Group Ltd
61–63 Uxbridge Road, London W5 5SA

Random House Inc
1540 Broadway, New York, New York 10036

Cover design: Darian Causby/Highway 51
Cover photography: Quentin Jones
Typeset in 12.5/17 Sabon by Midland Typesetters, Maryborough, Victoria
Printed and bound by Griffin Press, Netley, South Australia

10 9 8 7 6 5 4 3 2 1

To Joyce and Rex,
and to my father.

David Pescud, February 2003

Foreword

I MET DAVID PESCUD on Thursday, April 26, 2001, at the
launch of a television documentary for which I had
written the narration. It was about dyslexia and David,
who suffers from the condition so badly he can barely
read at all, was one of its subjects.

Standing in Foxtel's Green Room, quizzing this gruff,
mop-headed man, I realised his life story was nothing
short of extraordinary. This initial meeting left me
intrigued: how could someone like him achieve so much?
To help myself work it out, I wrote a profile of him for
The Weekend Australian Magazine. It was not a huge
article but the letters and emails it provoked were the kind
that journalists rarely see. Readers praised his bravery,
called him an inspiration and said his story should be sent
to every school and every parent in Australia.

One mother of two wrote: 'David, my boys love

sailing too. When they come home after school today, quickly finish their homework, grab a few slices of bread and run out the door to play, I'll be thinking of you. And when they go to bed tonight their bedtime story will be your story.'

It was then that David let on that people had been telling him for years that he should write his autobiography. This is a big ask for a man with his severe dyslexia – he can hardly write his own name and address. So he asked me if I would consider writing it instead.

What I had not realised until we were well underway was just how big a deal this was going to be for David. He has spent much of his life terrorised by the written word. He faced violence at school because he was unable to learn to read and has been emotionally hijacked by his illiteracy in ways I could never have imagined. He is a rough, tough, business-savvy guy, but underneath the bluff and bluster, this scared him witless.

The irony of writing a book about someone who will never be able to read it is not lost on either of us. Sure, David uses readers and scribes, but his access to the written word relies on trusting a third party, and trust does not always come easily.

David is by no means alone. During my research for the documentary, I realised that this condition, unrecognised when David was a child, may affect one in ten people in this country. Albert Einstein is believed to have suffered from it, as do Richard Branson, Tom Cruise and Cher. The science of it is not fully understood, but the effects of not being diagnosed are very clear.

Thanks are due to filmmaker Anna Bateman for introducing me to David in the first place, and to her son Azzam, whose own dyslexia sparked the whole thing off. Thank you Jane Southward at Random House for taking a punt on this story; Lyn Tranter for putting the deal together; and Keith Austin for making sure I didn't fall apart while I was putting the book together. Thanks also to present and former members of Sailors with disAbilities for use of photographs.

My mother tells me I taught myself to read when I was four. I don't believe her, but I am well aware that I have never known a world where the written word did not speak to me.

I take it for granted.

Having had the chance to get inside the head of David Pescud, I never will again.

Helen O'Neill, February 2003

1

ONE OF MY 'AUNTIES' who lived down the road takes great pleasure in telling anyone she can that when she first met Davey he was two years old, stark naked, pencil case in hand, heading north. Heading out of there. I have no idea what was going on in my tiny mind that day. All I knew was that no one was going to stop me. I've been like that pretty much ever since. Stubborn, pig-headed, crystal clear about where I'm going and why. And God help anybody who gets in my way.

Back then, in the early days before my brother and sister appeared on the scene, there was just me and my folks, and I was a Pescud alright – a blue-eyed, angel-faced, blond-headed, thickset, argumentative little sod. A carbon copy in body, brain and spirit of my father, Reginald Maxwell Pescud. Or so I thought.

Reg the Bugger, as he was affectionately known, met

my mother Joyce in 1940 when she was sixteen, he was seventeen, and World War II was well and truly under way. His older brother Harry was already in the air force on a tour of duty that would take him to Canada and England, and young Reg, who was kicking his heels as a clerk in the Bank of NSW and hating every minute of it, was desperate to get in on the action. The moment he hit eighteen, he signed up with the Royal Australian Air Force and off he went. Only as far as Brisbane, though, which, while being nearly 1000 kilometres north of the place Reg called home – the sleepy Sydney suburb of Punchbowl – was by no means far enough to keep him out of trouble. During those first few months, he went AWOL to see his girl so often he failed his pilotship and ended up training as an air gunner. Then a burst appendix almost took him out of the picture entirely. He recovered, but his future in the air force had been shot down in flames. His only option was to train up as a radar operator.

From the little Reg told the family later, he spent most of his war in the heart of New Guinea, the only Australian in a radar unit full of Americans who didn't understand his larrikin ways. While his colleagues were looking around for official ways to get things done, Reg was busy 'requisitioning' tables, chairs, beds, whatever the unit needed. He came into his own as a fixer and made sergeant fairly fast but even Reg could only do so much with the limited rations available, coming home on leave severely underweight and yellow from the malaria tablets that tropics-bound soldiers had to take. He was still in

Sydney when the war ended in August 1945, without him.

Under pressure from Joyce's parents – only a man with a steady job would do for their girl – Reg returned to the bank, to an office full of people whose own wars had largely been spent dotting i's and crossing t's. He loathed it but shrugged his shoulders, buckled down and made Joyce a June bride the following year, in a wedding short on luxuries but full of hope. Ration coupons were so thin on the ground that his best man, younger brother Les, had to borrow older brother Harry's suit.

I came into the picture on a Tuesday, September 2, 1947. It was a shocking birth, my mother delights in telling me: a long, painful labour for her and a nice Father's Day present for Reg. My arrival spurred him into action. Ignoring the frowns of Joyce's parents, he dumped the bank job and started up a chook farm. His chickens were happy enough – they had incubators, pens with nice, cosy warmers and no idea of the fate that would ultimately befall them – but they weren't very lucrative. Before too long Reg sold out and took another office job, with the Department of Air.

I didn't care. I was more concerned with the annoying and very sudden appearance of my small sister Bronwyn, just under two years later. Reg, meanwhile, was scouring the region for somewhere to settle, finding a patch of paradise down by the water in Yowie Bay, Sutherland Shire, one of Sydney's southern suburbs. He talked it over with Joyce, borrowed much more than the two of them could really afford, and bought it. This was where my childhood really began, in a rundown shack just this side of being habitable. There was nothing there but bush and bay: we could roam pretty much unhindered by any kind of man-made obstacle as far as we liked south, east and west, and the only defining thing was water.

A thin bitumen road running along a ridge about 150 metres above the cool, deep bay took visitors to our drive, which led them down the slope to our ramshackle home. Beneath the house was a long narrow stretch of land that raced straight down to the rocks beneath. The setting was absolutely breathtaking. Which was probably just as well, because inside what we laughingly called 'our house' was utter turmoil. Built as a fisherman's weekender, it could barely have been more basic. There was no hot water, no inside toilet, no bathroom and a fuel stove hungry for wood that had to be chopped every weekend.

Reg renovated in instalments, as and when he could afford to, but every time he completed one job, a new one reared up to take its place. Those renovations went on for most of my childhood and at some stage I started to realise that Dad would never really finish them. He got more involved with work – starting social clubs, organising Christmas parties for the workers' children and establishing himself as the person people would come to with their problems – and the house just stood there, gently mocking him; a dilapidated monster he could never fully tame.

The quest to keep us clean caused no end of trouble. Early on, washtime meant sitting in a galvanised tin bath, waiting for Mum to put our screwed-up, soapy

4

faces out of their misery by emptying jugs of water all over our heads. Reg and my mother managed to save enough to replace it with an enamelled cast iron number, a big step up, and as the weekend approached, we kids were all revved up. Until Friday night, when Reg got home and announced that he had given all the money for the bath to some bloke from work – my mother swears it was because he needed it, but Dad later told me the guy had dropped the entire bundle on a horse. Either way, we had to wait.

There were celebrations all round when Dad finally got a hot water system installed. It ran off the fuel stove but he had it connected to a tank in the roof and the plumbing was not right. Getting hot water for a bath was easy enough: you just turned the heating system on and waited for a while. Trickier was remembering to turn it back off. Those who didn't learnt the hard way, after the roof tank flooded the living room below; very handy in wintertime when we would come in from sailing, light the fire in the living room and quite frequently set fire to the house.

The roof had holes in it but Dad would invariably say, 'Don't worry about it. It only leaks when it rains.' Great, I'd think, peeling off my sopping wet socks and trying to find a dry spot to hang them. Why doesn't he just fix the bloody thing? He always found time for us, though, building treehouses, and a cubby inside what was left of an old water tank on the property, for my sister and me. If we wanted to make a boat, he would invariably be there, cutting up corrugated iron and helping us hammer it together to fashion some kind of rudimentary hull. When my mates and I cowered in terror behind our Eureka Stockade, at war with the banksia men, Dad would be right up there with us, dressed in nothing but a pair of tatty shorts, firing at the imaginary enemy. My father was one of us but he was also more than that. He was outspoken, unshakeable and an awful lot of fun, full of stories of history and romance. He told tall tales and played games that connected our pint-sized world with the real one. He made things relevant.

Life was always an adventure around Dad and I wanted to be just like him. There was only one problem. Unlike my father, who moved with a lithe, feline grace and could scale the steepest of slopes like a misplaced mountain goat, I was incredibly accident prone. It didn't occur to any of us for decades that this might be a sign that there was something fundamentally wrong with me, that my terrible hand–eye coordination and lack of balance pointed to some kind of bad wiring in my brain. This went way beyond the normal narrow scrapes most boys with enquiring minds put their parents through, such as cutting through a live, plugged-in electric light cord with scissors just to see what would happen (nothing, luckily). Instead, I was in and out of the doctor's office every other week getting stitch after stitch after stitch. I have no idea to this day how many I have on my head alone.

The first event I can recall happened when I was three, at my grandparents' house. For no apparent reason I went careering into a table my great-grandfather had built, leaving a dent in the woodwork and a lovely series of stitches running down the left side of my face. About a month later I came off a tree swing and ended up with a matching set on the right. Anywhere a kid could hurt themselves, I did, ending up eternally covered in scratches and bruises. Within about an hour of most birthday parties, be they Bronwyn's or my own, I would be on my way to the doctor's surgery for more emergency treatment, having fallen over my own shadow in excitement or tumbled off a small cliff.

One day I was messing around with a huge earthenware pot that was lying outside. One corner of our house sat over the creek and I wanted to move the pot into the water to create a dam and hydro system. I got Bronwyn to help me push the pot along while I was pulling it, but we were on a slope and soon the whole thing came down on top of my ankle, crushing it so badly I still have pieces of pot in my leg. So, back into hospital again, getting another twenty-four stitches and a telling-off for not being careful.

Before long, the doctors told my mother that I had had so many cuts, scratches, stitches and bangs, they reckoned that if I didn't get a course of tetanus shots, I would end up dying of it. 'You're the first kid in New South Wales to have the full course,' the nurse said sweetly, readying her long, steel needle. I closed my eyes and waited for the world to stop turning.

The accident no one lets me forget happened because our house lay halfway down a very steep hill. By the time I was in primary school, I was riding my pushbike to school. A favourite bet between my knuckleheaded mates and me was that I could not ride all the way back from school to home without touching the handlebars or brakes. It wasn't the longest of trips but bang-slap in the middle of it there was quite a big hill which took you down one avenue and shot you up the other side. Then you had to negotiate a corner before you hit another hill which dropped straight down into our drive. From there the track levelled out to a flat section where our garage was, then dropped away over a cliff that dived the 10 metres or so straight into the bay below. It was a test of nerves more than anything. The key was keeping your hands up as long as possible while cleverly avoiding plunging to your doom.

On that fateful day, I was going well. I didn't touch the brakes until I was three-quarters of the way down our drive, by which time I was scooting along faster than I had ever travelled in my life. It had been raining, so when I did slam on the brakes – with a mixture of panic and annoyance for not managing to get all the way to the end – the damn things didn't work. I hurtled down this hill hell for leather past all the bush and trees, looking at the bottom and knowing there was a cliff and then metres and metres of nothing before I hit the rocks and water.

As I came down into the final straight, I careered past our garage and over the cliff. I was airborne. I sailed past a tree and in total reflex panic grabbed hold of a branch. When Mum came out a few minutes later I was hanging on for grim death nearly five metres above the ground with my legs wrapped around my pushy – I didn't want to drop it in case I buckled the back wheel. I don't remember getting down but I do recall the bike was okay, as I was, for once. Only my dignity took a knock that day.

What was becoming increasingly clear to everyone was that I, unlike most kids, was much safer in the water than on dry land. That suited me fine: the water had been beckoning for as long as I could remember. It was exactly where I wanted to be. Until I learnt to swim, a turpentine tree stood between me and happiness – the tree was rooted fast halfway between our house and the water. One of our parents' unshakeable rules was that Bronwyn and I weren't allowed to go past it until we could swim.

Beneath the house, by the rocks, we had what we called our swimming pool: a set of rough stairs leading to a whitewashed indent in the foreshore with some timber secured round the perimeter and wire shoved in the sand to keep the sharks out. I used to jump off the steps, struggle out into the pool with a couple of strokes, then scramble back to the side. The first time I made it from one side to the other I was off. There was suddenly no reason for not doing absolutely anything, and to my parents' credit there were no real limitations put on that freedom for me or my sister, once she had learnt to swim as well.

Mum always had a fresh, round loaf of bread in the kitchen and we would come home from school, cut some big hunks of bread, whack margarine on them, cover the lot in honey, and be off. We tore out of the house, shedding clothes, shirts and satchels on the way; then whoosh, we were gone. We wouldn't come back until dark. Summertime was heaven on a stick. There always seemed to be a new adventure, another frontier. Tree-houses to build, haunted houses to explore, new places to stash our secrets.

As soon as I got freedom of the boats my father had tethered in our family moorings, I would be out – on rowboats, sailboats, whatever floating object I could find. With my mate Alan Cooper, who lived a few doors across, I soon worked out how to build makeshift vessels by finding a sheet of corrugated iron, stomping on it to flatten it out, bending the two ends up together, slamming a long, straight piece of wood into the middle and securing the construction together with rope. Hey presto! A tin canoe. We would strap two of these together to make catamarans, paddle out to the Bay Surf – a line of swell where the bay water meets that of the ocean – and then surf back in to land in these things, which would go down like a stone as soon as they hit the wrong angle in the water.

Alan and I did this all day, and when night-time fell, if we were too far from home to stumble back in the dark, we would sleep on the nearest beach and make our way home at daybreak. My parents were never worried. By nine years old I was a better bushman than most people ever become, and I was very responsible for my age, so they just let us go. And go we did.

Every weekend I could, I would run off with Alan – or Georgie or Keith, who also lived nearby. We were being fed on World War II with our fathers having been in the battles, and we all thought we were Jungle Jim, GI Joe, you name it. We would tell our folks we were off for a hike in the National Park which lay across the bay, chuck a few provisions in the rowboat, scoot across the water and come back two days later. We didn't have tents so we slept in any spot we could find, eating anything we could lay our hands on. Oysters, which grew all over the rocks, were a favourite. If you had a knife you could get a good feed by prising them off and open. If you didn't, you would just grab some dry tinder from the bush floor, wait until low tide, drape it over the oysters and light it. They popped open in terror and we scooped them out and swallowed them.

Things did not always work as I intended. One morning during school holidays I got up really early and shot over to Keith's place to check we were still on for the trip. He lived a couple of houses down through the bush, and when I got there, yes, we were on, and he was as excited as I was. By the time I made it back to my place, my old man was standing there waiting for me, with a face as black as thunder. My job was to collect the milk every morning from a billy can we left at the top of the drive that was filled every morning by the milkman. I hadn't done it. Grounded.

The others came over about half an hour later, ready for our expedition. I was the one who had the makeshift fishing and camping gear we used.

'Let's go,' Keith called out from the back of the house.

'I can't, I'm stuck,' I said. 'You can though.' So I gave them all my stuff and the rowboat tethered to our mooring, and trudged back up the hill to the house as they splashed their way across the bay.

That night when Dad came home, he brought a Swiss army-style knife for me. It had all sorts of things hidden in it, everything from a magnifying glass to a toasting fork. I couldn't believe it. That morning he grounded me; that night he brought me home the kind of present little boys dream of. I just could not figure it out. Mum explained things later. Apparently she had rung him at work and told him that I had given all my stuff to my friends so they could go off. The old man was awash with guilt and got this thing, which he probably couldn't afford. I could have kissed him.

I learnt much during those childhood adventures but met nothing on them that ever scared me. Indeed, the first time I saw fear in somebody else, I was really surprised. It was one of my friends, Alan, and we were out hiking. Our families had camped out at Jibbon Beach, a boat-ride across the bay to the fringes of the National Park, and we disappeared off by boat to another beach the moment we could get away. We parked our boat on a beach and walked across an isthmus to get to the ocean on the other side.

In those days the area had a few humpies, little huts people used to live in with their dogs and horses. It was cowboy land. We were haring around like mad things and a woman stuck her head out of her door and screamed out at us to get lost and never come down this way again. We giggled but said to each other, okay, we'll walk around the rocks and see if we can get back to the boat that way. Before too long we were hopelessly lost, locked out by the ocean and the scrub.

Then Alan went and stood on an ant heap. He was getting bitten alive and he went into panic mode. Maybe if I'd been standing on the ant heap I'd have reacted that way too, but I wasn't. He got completely hysterical and I remember looking at him, frowning, and saying, 'Hey, come on, it'll be alright,' while I tried to brush the ants off. 'Calm down,' I told him. 'We'll find the boat. We'll just walk back another way. It's going to be okay.' That was also the first time that I realised you can control fear. It was a good lesson to learn early on.

Every day brought something new and the over-whelming sense was always 'we can do that', whether we could or not. We can build a raft. We can build a tin canoe. We can paddle it out to the Bay Surf; we can bring it back in. We would be rowing about all day fishing for blackfish and garfish – with varying degress of success – and we would not see anybody for hours on end. Bends in the river, bush rising all around, silent except for the noises of the water, the birds, the fish jumping. Angophoras that seemed to stretch forever. The bush was full of wallabies, possums and deer, but I was not too bothered about them. I used to sit in the boat trying to imagine what it was like when the Aborigines were here. Not too different, was the conclusion I came to.

As we explored the endless nooks and crannies of Port Hacking, we got to know the denizens of the deep pretty well. One favourite was the oversized turtle that lived under a rock ledge and would poke its big, timid head up to the surface if you stayed very still and threw the right kind of bait about.

Every now and again I would bring a handspear and watch the bait fish ripple to see where the larger fish were moving them. The place was teeming with stingrays, gropers and sharks, of course. Alan and I used to capture stingrays that were about a metre across. I don't know what we thought we would do with them but we dropped a spear into them, the line would snap and the poor things would rush off with the spear in their backs. We never managed to land one.

The king of this domain was an old two-metre grey nurse shark who lived up at the point. Our game was to bait him by fishing above the depths we thought he was lurking in, and then try and whisk our catch back up into our rickety boat before Jaws bit all but the hooked heads off them. It didn't often work. Dad had a shark rig but he'd never managed to catch the old beast. We were forbidden to even try. So one day, one of my mates and I went to the butcher's, bought ourselves a bucketful of blood and some ox hearts and snuck out in our boat to the shark's lair.

Adrenalin pumping, we tipped the bucket of blood into the water with our excited, sweaty hands, and chucked all but one of the hearts overboard into the red, receding mess. We threaded the last ox heart on a big, mean-looking hook attached to a long steel cable. On the end of that was a five-gallon drum, then a line from the drum to the boat itself. The idea was that the shark would take the heart, swallow the hook and head back down to his lair, fighting the drum so we would not have to fight him. The drum would take the sting out of him, tiring him out until we could catch him and finish him off. Well, we sat there for hours waiting for the shark to take the bait. Hours and hours. Rapt attention turned into thumb-twiddling boredom. We trailed our hands in the water, ate our sandwiches, told jokes and kicked the side of the boat to see how far the ripples would go.

As twilight fell, we decided to pull the rig out and just as we leant over, BANG! The shark took the bait, knocking us flat on our backs and taking our little boat screaming across the water. We hung on for grim death, clawing our way up to the front where the rig was. If the five-gallon drum was causing old Jaws any trouble, he wasn't showing it. His pace did not slacken at all. He pulled us one way, then another, then dived down, then came back up, throwing us off our feet at every turn. The sensible thing to do was to cut the rope, but that wasn't going to happen because we'd lose Dad's rig and then we really would have been in trouble. By the time it was pitch-black we plucked up the courage and sliced across the securing ropes with the knife my Dad had bought me. The whole lot disappeared into the deep. We never did find out what happened to the shark. I would like to think he spat out the hook and never gave us another thought. Whatever, we never saw him again.

Real fishing was for the men. Unlike us, they were allowed to head off outside the rivers into the ocean, which they seemed to do every weekend without us. Early in the morning my uncles would come down, join forces with my dad, and get the boat out before the sun was even up and anyone else was awake. They'd come back at eleven or twelve with their catch – sometimes a boatful, sometimes just a few choice fish – then they'd enact a ritual in which they'd spread all the fish out under the mulberry tree and argue about who got which and why.

Next came the row about who was going to pay for petrol – they'd sit there having a beer for at least an hour discussing who was going to do this. 'No, no, no,' it would go. 'It's my turn. You bought the beer with Harry.' It just went on – any excuse to sit there in the shade, and tell lies, and talk about fishing. My gang would sit on the edge of that circle trying to be part of it. We dressed the same – in shorts, and old T-shirts – trying to edge in. Always sidling nearer, but never getting quite close enough.

The first time I was allowed to go with Dad, just me and him together, it felt like a rite of passage. For some reason it was late, about 5 am, and daylight when we finally got the boat out, but by the time we made it into Bate Bay a few hours away, we hooked into fish, thousands of them. I could catch fish out of a gutter in those days, and while we motored along I had torn up some devon and used it to pick up a couple of spiny mackerel, which I chopped up for bait as well.

We hooked into a big drift of flathead, just the two of us with two lines. Dad cut strips of mackerel, banged them on hooks and threw them over the side while I'd go around from one line to the next pulling up fish, over and over again, because fish was food, and food was money, and we didn't have any money. We were pulling the slimy, flapping creatures up like nobody's business. I couldn't go any faster. We came back into port when the boat was chock-a-block with fish, and I was so proud.

Before we were allowed to use the sailboat, my mates and I converted our rowboat into a Viking ship by sticking a mast in the middle, then making sails out of anything – old sheets, canvas, curtains. Anything. And we were gone. As the breeze blew down the bay, we would row until we were tucked into one of the cliffs under the hills, put our mast up, set our sail, row out to the line of the wind and away we'd go. We would scream down to Yowie Bay, row back and do it again and again, until the boat was in pieces. Then we'd pick up those pieces, drag them to the boat shed and stick the whole thing back together again.

I thought it was perfectly normal to spend your days chasing fish and your nights charging through the bush on some mission. We had cubbyhouses, treehouses, and endless wars with banksia men. It was marvellous and I assumed everyone lived like that. We didn't have any money, we were stony, more or less. But we had a launch, we had a rowboat, we probably had a couple of sailboats in the boat shed in various states of repair. We had a swimming pool, we had fishing tackle. To my mind we had everything, and what we didn't have we could make.

The day I realised not everyone lived like that came when I was about nine years old. Television had just hit, so I guess it must have been about 1957, and everyone was busy buying the new sets. Everyone, it seemed, but us – there was no way we could afford it. I was already having trouble with reading at school, so my classmates knew me as Davey the Dickhead. It didn't matter too much to me – I lived in my world of boats and everything else could go to hell. But this one kid was trying to rile me in the classroom one day before the final bell went. In an attempt to get him off my back I said, 'Oh shut up. We've got a television set, so there.'

'Oh yeah?' he said, sneering at me. 'I wanna see it.'

Now, he lived near the school and we lived a fair way from it so I just thought, oh, it'll never happen, because you're a lazy little sod and it's a long ride on your pushy. We all had these beaten-up pushbikes and I thought there was no way this kid was going to ride all the way to my house on his. Only the little bugger did. He collared me one afternoon and followed me home, all the way. I was in such a panic. What the hell was I going to show him? And what was I going to get called the next day at school? Brilliant, I thought. Tomorrow not only am I going to be called a dumbo and a dickhead, all the kids will know I'm a liar as well. My parents had a wind-up gramophone and in my panicked confusion I thought, I'll show him that.

As we walked towards the house with its big glass windows, he caught a glimpse of the bushland and the sparkling, shimmering blue beneath it. 'Do you live on the water?' he said.

I was two paces inside the back door, still thinking,

oh shit, and there he was babbling on about the water. I said, 'Yes, of course we do. So what?'

'Have you got a boat?' came the question.

'Er, yeah.'

'Are you allowed to go out on the boat?'

'Course I am.'

'Can we go out on the boat? Like, now?'

I was still trying to work out what I was going to do about this TV we didn't have, but he was so excited about the boat he completely forgot about the television. I checked if he could swim and the penny dropped. I was off the hook. We whizzed down to the water, into the rowboat and off we went. He never mentioned the television again.

A little while after that it started to sink in that the way I lived my life was different to other kids, and that I had something they only dreamt of.

I lived in a world of stingrays and sharks and bream and rowboats – going to bed of a night with my hands stinking of fish guts and stinging with rope burns, and not really worrying about a thing. It was boats and bush and freedom. If it sounds like paradise, that is because it was. My home life back then really did seem like heaven to me.

My school life, on the other hand, was hell.

2

My first kindie teacher, Miss Jacobs, was the best thing since sliced bread. She was kind, sweet, blonde and gorgeous – I was in love. It was when I made the move to primary school that my problems began.

Numbers were never too difficult – I could see them and work with them fairly easily, although anyone who watched me copying them down would quickly spot that I was probably doing it backwards. Building letters into words was a whole other ball game. Every time my teacher asked me to open a reading book, my heart sank. It's the same today. Every word on the page moves around – nothing stays still. The printed symbols start running into each other, slithering their way into the margins, compressing. Then they will suddenly separate. I would see patterns that were not there. The white gaps running down the page between words looked like deliberate images to me; and they moved, like thin trickles of water picking their way downhill through a landscape of black, misshapen boulders.

The other kids didn't know what I was talking about when I tried to explain it to them, but when I looked at a page of typewritten passages, I couldn't see anything meaningful. The words we were straining to decipher remained unfathomable hieroglyphs. I could look at the white paper – some people with my condition find the glare too much even to do that – but no matter how much I battled with the letters in front of me, they refused to release their secrets.

Most children have something in their brains that makes learning how to read and write almost instinctive. It was becoming very clear that I did not. I had to think about every single word I tried to read. I never got headaches, but the concentration required to make any meaning bleed through the pages left me utterly exhausted. Even the simple copying of letters, words and sentences was not straightforward. I would fashion the letters back to front, or in jumbled mirror images. No matter how hard I tried, they would not come out right.

At first this wasn't too much of an issue; all it meant was that I was lagging a little behind the other kids my age. They were turning d-o-g into happy little puppies with wagging tales that could run off and play with imaginary sticks. There were no such games for me; I was losing myself between the gaps in the words. My teachers' first reaction was to go back to the drawing board with me, in an attempt to work through the problems more slowly, trying to make me understand where it was I was going wrong. 'He's a bright enough child, he is bound to catch on,' they told my parents. They were wrong.

The years dragged on, punctuated by the odd eye test to work out if perhaps I needed glasses. No, that wasn't it either. There were glimmers of hope when I developed an ability to remember certain words. They tended to be those I could visualise, such as c-h-a-i-r, t-o-e and d-e-s-k. If I could do that, I thought to myself, maybe I could lever open the d-o-o-r to everything else with inspired guessing. No, I could not. The method only worked for a few, quite simple words. Anything longer and I was in trouble.

The other kids were all taking a different tack. They could somehow work out a word by building it up, letter by letter, syllable by syllable. Stu-pid. Thick-head. I could never learn to do that. By the time I would get to the final syllable, I'd have forgotten what the first one was. Even so, I held out hope for entire sentences. When our textbook said 'The girl sat in the chair' I knew there would be a logic to it. I pushed my finger along each word and could sometimes make out 'g-i-r-l . . . s-a-t . . .'; then I'd see the c-h and guess the word 'chair'. But by the time I'd got to the first few letters of the following word, everything in the sentence was going blurry and jiggling around. I could not hold the early letters still on the page and then, because everything started moving, I lost the word and had to abandon hope of making any sense of the sentence. There was another minefield too. Even the few shorter words I could remember well enough to read, I would not be able to spell. Even 'chair', one of my few successes, would sometimes come out completely backwards.

Numbers were never quite such a problem because the teachers writing down problems on the blackboard would invariably talk their way through it to make sure the class was paying attention. If I could hear it, I could remember it, and I learnt to do calculations in my head, building mathematical maps in my mind that bypassed the need for pen and paper. I could not write things down but if the teacher jumped on me in class, there was a fair chance I would know how to answer the question. It didn't save me, though. I spent my first attempt to get through one particular year standing in the corner, facing the wall, having failed, yet again, to do anything right. It was miserable but I could handle it, even though I didn't understand what was making me so different from the other kids.

The solution to my quandary appeared simple to the school. I would just have to go through the entire year again, with a bunch of much smaller kids and a new teacher, Mr Blake (whose real name I cannot use for legal reasons). His approach was different to anything I had encountered before. He seemed to think I was doing this on purpose. He forced me to stand up and try to read passages of text out loud in front of the class, and when it became clear I couldn't even stammer my way through the first few words, he would hurl abuse at me: 'Pescud, you're a slob . . . You're lazy . . . You're useless . . . Oh shut up, you idiot boy, and take this. Even a moron like you can read what's written there.'

He handed me a tall, pointed hat with the word DUNCE painted on it. I had to put it on my head and stand in the classroom corner, facing the wall, while everyone else skipped and giggled their way through the passages I could not penetrate. Sure, my classmates would stumble over the odd unfamiliar word, but every one of them could make their way through it. I didn't understand what was going on.

Those lessons left me burning with shame but I always knew worse was to come. When the bell rang and we all ran out of class, however fast I fled I could never escape the taunts from the other kids, parroting the abuse Mr Blake had taught them.

'Stupid slob.'

'Pathetic Pescud.'

'Davey Dickhead.'

It wasn't long before Mr Blake upped the ante. At least once a week he began calling me to the front of my class so he could cane me for wilfully 'refusing' to learn to read. He used a 15-inch ruler with a brass edge running down one side. I was terrified of that piece of metal. I used to have nightmares about it. Mr Blake would call me a 'fat slob', 'lazy', 'thick' – any negative descriptions he could think of he threw at me in front of everybody else while the ruler came down over and over again on the palm of my hand. I bit back the tears while Mr Blake let me and the rest of my class know in no uncertain terms that I was 'useless' and 'unbelievably stupid': 'Pescud, you will never learn,' he told me. 'Ever.'

Winter, summer, there was no difference. The only change came when my teacher ran out of insults. On those occasions, he caned me in silence while chewing his false teeth. He had a plate which he used to drop out of his mouth slightly as he was slicing the ruler down into my bare, open hand, again and again, until he was finished and I was allowed to walk to the classroom corner burning with shame. Then I would put the DUNCE hat on again and spend the rest of the lesson with my back to everybody.

By this stage my problems at school were starting to infect my whole life. Poor old Mum and Dad had no idea what to do. Both were working class people bright enough to win selective high school places, and they had no reason to think I wouldn't be like them. They knew I could put six and seven together pretty fast in my head, but neither of them could work out why I couldn't understand the words set out clearly in front of me. The teachers weren't much help. 'He's just a little late maturing' was the best they could get out of them.

As far as Mum was concerned, it set me apart. She started comparing me to other kids we knew, which for me just reinforced the whole disaster. Looking back, I wonder if she and Dad had a kind of good guy, bad guy routine mapped out. He was always having fun with us. She was the one who forced me to sit down and try to make the words speak to me. It was always Mum telling me to do my homework, badgering me about why I couldn't complete it, why I did not appear even to try. One time we were doing maths and she kept telling me to 'read' the problem. As soon as she said that word 'read', I froze. Those little squiggles in front of me were numbers, not letters. What did she mean, 'read' them? You read words, you don't read numbers.

The whole thing became so emotional for me that everything jammed, which it still does today. Nothing works: no logic, no rationale. It all just stops. Give me a piece of paper covered in print even now and I have to breathe deeply to push the panic away. Sit me in a room quietly alone, where I can run my finger across a page without anybody watching me, and I'll probably be able to pick my way through a sentence. Put me under pressure and I explode. Envelopes terrify me – I've got more unopened letters than most people have had hot dinners. I'm too scared to open them. At over fifty years of age, I'm still too scared.

It was back then, with my mother, that I began to really lose my way. Trying to read was like entering a maze that I could never get out of. I was lost and frustrated and cranky. Mr Blake rammed this home to me every Thursday afternoon. That was the day he set spelling tests. They were hell. We would copy down lists of twenty words from the blackboard and take them home to learn by rote for the test the following morning. I sat at the kitchen table in terror, trying to pound the shapes into my skull until my brain felt like it would bleed from the effort.

One Thursday I worked through the list with Mum. We pored over the words, drilling each again and again until I finally thought I had nailed every single one.

'Cement' caused me particular trouble – did it start with an 's'? Where did the e's go? We battered away at it until I thought I had really learnt it. Success.

I got up the next morning but it was a blank. I knew it was 'c', then 'e', then I'd lose it and it would come out 'semt'. I just could not see the word. The letters ran away from me. There was no way I could build the word. I shuffled onto my chair with an impending sense of doom. As Mr Blake called out the words, I wrote my answers down, knowing there was nothing I could do.

Sure enough, I'd spelt them all wrong. As soon as Mr Blake had finished marking them, he called me up to the front of the class for yet another caning. I was used to it by then – I had been caned so many times for so many offences. But as I walked up to meet my punishment and stood there vainly attempting to keep my eyes open to stop myself from crying, it all seemed incredibly unfair. I had tried so hard to get it right, and what had happened? I had failed again. There was something wrong with me. It wasn't that I couldn't read, it was that I couldn't learn. The cuts came raining down onto my trembling palm. It was one of those occasions when Mr Blake seemed happy enough with his own thoughts and didn't even bother abusing me. Maybe he didn't think I was worth it.

When it was all over I walked back to my desk, sat down and tried to pick up a pencil. I ran my shaking finger slowly down my answer-sheet. Cross, cross, cross. Finally I found the mark where I had tried to write 'cement'. Looking at that cross just killed me. It was probably around that time that I gave up. I didn't want to play this game any more. Mr Blake was right: I was a failure, and I was a dickhead. That Pescud kid was never going to learn anything, he was too stupid. I knew this for a fact, just like I knew grass was green.

There was no let-up at school: not being able to read and write cut me out of every lesson except physical education. History, geography, biology and maths were closed books, literally as well as metaphorically. I could follow a graphic on a blackboard, but tell me to check a textbook and you were locking me out of everything the education system claimed to offer. My school rewarded my utter failure by appointing me its 'Chief Incinerator Lighter', the job given to the stupidest child considered responsible enough to do it. Duties included spending part of the school day collecting rubbish from the bins dotted around the school grounds, and dumping everybody else's garbage in the incinerator. To this day the smell of orange peel still gives me the shivers.

At home I began crying myself to sleep almost every night. Other children dreamt of turning themselves into wildlife photographers, astronauts and surgeons, picking role models out of the books and magazines they leafed through so easily. I had a role model too. He was the sewage collector who visited our house once a week to pick up what we called the dunny pan before we got connected up to the main sewerage works and I knew that when I grew up I would be a dunny man too. I was not fit to do anything else.

Late in primary school I started swimming for the school. Finally, something I was good at, but even that was rife with confusion – one day I was getting whacked, the next I was standing up on the dais with everyone clapping.

Not being able to read threw everything into relief. Bronwyn was two years younger than me so until then she was always the one trying to keep up with what I was doing. I was bigger, stronger, more coordinated, having every adventure under the sun, and pretty dismissive of her. She'd follow me and Dad around when we were doing things like unscrewing the water pipes that ran down to our house – something that had to be done every year to control the rust – so big Pescud and little Pescud would be there, dressed exactly the same, working away. Then Bronnie would appear, sucking her thumb, tucking her wavy hair into the side of her mouth. She'd want to join in – until it actually came to it, and she would bottle out. I would laugh to myself. She's just a girl, I would think with a sneer.

That all changed when she turned out to be a compulsive reader. She never had her head out of a book and suddenly she shot in front of me. She was finding out about things I could only dream of. My world was what I heard and what I saw. Hers was teeming with everything that books could bring to her. I don't think she meant to lord her literacy over me, but it became a festering sore. I knew exactly why she could open a book and make sense of it while I could not. It was because she was clever and I was stupid. I trashed the Enid Blyton meetings she held with her friends in the cubbyhouse, but it didn't change the facts of our family. Bronwyn was smart like my parents, and I was dumb. Davey Dick-head, so stupid his kid sister can do things he can't. That stupid idiot David Pescud. So thick he can't even read. Fit for nothing but work as a dunny man. End of story.

Every day I would drag myself into my white, green, grey and orange uniform – the colour of the bottlebrush, our head teacher told us with delight – and trudge into school. Every night I would fly back to paradise and the water. There, as I rowed furiously into the middle of my waterways, everything melted away. There was no one calling me names, no one having a go at me. None of the creatures there knew how stupid I was. It didn't matter that I couldn't read books. I would spend hour after hour learning how to read the water.

I drifted with the current, spending what felt like forever with my nose to the water, watching what was going on underneath my boat. Bubbles trailed up to the surface, and I worked out what creatures – fish, snakes, slow-lunged birds, insects – were down there and which was chasing what. Birds fascinated me: I watched sea eagles catching the wind's edge with an effortlessness it would take me decades to even start mastering, and I learnt that when a bird is sitting on the water's surface, it means something. He's never there for luck, he's chasing fish. In nature there is always a reason for what you're seeing. My own efforts at catching food were less elegant but my lines were, like everything, beautifully simple: a piece of nylon wrapped around a Coke bottle with a hook. I'd smash some oysters to get bait, or chop up any little piece of food I'd stuffed into my pockets.

I caught enough fish to keep Mum happy.

It was around this time that Port Hacking Sailing Club was built, right across the bay from our house. My father must have decided it would be a good thing for me to get involved in, and Alan Cooper and I ended up going over there while it was being built and volunteered to nail boards onto the building as the structure went up. This is where I learnt the basics of sailboat racing, scooting around closed courses on the bay in fleets every Sunday morning. Alan and I started out in VJs, a small, two-man class of boat, and before long both our boat-houses were playing host to boats belonging to other people who wanted them near the sailing club but who were not lucky enough to have waterfront properties. The father of one such friend, Rob, had an old, fairly heavy VJ called *Sugar*, and it was on that boat that I started realising what sailing was all about.

Sugar had cotton sails and manila, layered rope. Woven ropes were beyond us back then but I do remember when we got our first decent spinnaker. It might have been nylon, I can't quite recall, but it was a great improvement because usually when Rob and I tipped the boat over and went upside down into the drink, the sail would become so waterlogged we would be drying it out for hours. Until we fell over again, usually. The flash new spinnaker put paid to all that. Water simply flew off it. Unfortunately it did not stop us arguing.

I was a surly sailor even then, kicking up a huge fuss if I could not be the skipper, and I burnt through several friendships that might have been quite useful otherwise.

But it opened up a whole new passion in me for the bay. And for the ocean that lay beyond. When things got really rough at school I would just come down to the boathouse, jump in whatever was tethered there, and leave everything behind. Nothing mattered on the water. There, nothing could harm me. It only ever calmed me.

School firmly became somewhere I did not want to be. I would race home, rain or shine, only to find my mother sitting on the back porch, on a lounge chair that my father had made her. Some afternoons she would still be in her dressing gown and nightie, surrounded by books and empty teacups. She would have been reading all day. She came from a very conventional home; her father had worked as a carriage builder at the railways. Then she met my dad, a strong, independent thinker who went off to the war, came back with new ideas and together they went on this learning curve about life, the universe and everything.

By 1959 Dad had left his job at the Department of Air and become a parole officer, diving into a psychology course at university that was prising open the criminal mind for him. He helped place prisoners in jobs during the day, and studied at night. The more he learnt, the more he wanted to know about the world, and that thirst for knowledge blossomed in Mum as well. He was discovering literature and bringing it home to Mum, who raced through classics such as *The Grapes of Wrath* and *The Well of Loneliness*. A new world was opening up in front of them – new friends, new influences, new thoughts. Pristine and second-hand books were always lying around the house, clumped beside chairs with their indecipherable spines laughing at me. I would pick them up and look at the cover, but as for opening them and trying to read them – what was the point? The irony was that I loved books. I loved the smell, the feel of them. I couldn't read them but I desperately wanted to know what they held that I could never get to.

When I came home after a caning to see that Mum's head had been in a book all day, I never asked her what she was reading. I just grabbed my few slices of bread and ran down to the water. Our little launch was tied up to the wharf down there. As kids we used to sit on it while we were winding it back into the boat shed, until one day the cable broke and shot us out into Yowie Bay. I was the biggest kid out there, so I picked up the heavy old oars and rowed us back to the shore. After we'd tied the launch up to the wharf, Dad took me aside and said, 'You did a really good job of that, David.' That moment of praise sticks in my mind because it didn't seem to happen much in my life. There was so much negative stuff going on that I clung to any good scrap that was thrown at me.

Dad used to read to me a lot before it became clear I would never be able to read for myself. Those first books were *The Wind in the Willows*, Banjo Paterson and CJ Dennis, but really, I lived for the radio – a little bakelite thing with the front broken off which was araldited onto the ABC. From five to six most evenings, it was children's hour featuring *The Argonauts*, a magical show full of music and stories so vividly told you felt you were actually there. I heard those tales in 3D technicolour. I don't think I ever wanted to live someone else's life; I would sit there hearing these incredible tales and think, how could I do that? If I were Ernest Shackleton about to embark on my trip to the Antarctic, what would I take? How would I store it? Would I make it back? Sure, I was destined to be a dunny man, but something else niggled at me. I wanted adventure, and not just second-hand. Of all the stories I was hearing, the most interesting one to me was the one I could achieve, the adventure I could have. Every time a strange boat came into the bay I would jump in the rowboat, grab the splintering oars and zoom out to meet it.

I was out on the water one sunny afternoon with Dad when the first decent yacht I'd ever seen sailed majestically into our waters. She was a beautiful vessel, about 28 or 30 feet long, a cutter rig with an exceptional swing to her shearline – that long, elegant line of the boat that carries it along the waterline. She was a cream colour with a timber superstructure and a varnished Oregon mast. I had heard about boats that looked like that but I had never seen one until that day. I was stunned. The boat moored in the bay and we rowed our way around it. I was running the skiff and the old man was in there with me. We rested the oars in the water and looked out along them to the beautiful creature beyond, the water so still that the drips coming off my oars shattered the boat's perfect reflection.

'I bet I could go to New Zealand in that,' I whispered to my father.

'Yes, son, you could,' he replied. 'A boat like that could take you anywhere.'

3

IT WAS NEW YEAR'S EVE, 1961, and the family was out on a camping expedition, something we did a lot. That year we had set up camp with the Cooper family and celebrated Christmas at a lovely spot in Cobbitty, out on the south-west fringes of Sydney by a dogleg in the Nepean River. The Coopers were fantastic. They lived about six houses away and had a boy a year older than me – my friend Alan – and a girl a year older than Bronwyn. Ken Cooper was great pals with my dad; they fished together most weekends and belonged to the same Masonic Lodge in Caringbah, although they annoyingly would never tell us anything about it.

My father was exhausted. He was working during the day and studying at night, and he needed a break – the rest of us were just along for the ride. There was Mum, Dad, me, my sister Bronwyn and my younger brother Mark,

who was six. We'd pitched camp with our little tents and
Mum and Dad's caravan in a cow paddock near the river.
It was a lovely spot, quiet and green – felt like a million
miles from anywhere. And it was one of those hot, wet
summers. When the rain came it was torrential, though
being soaked to the skin didn't stop us doing anything. We
would just hare around in the wet instead of the dry. Alan
and I had worked out that we could cross behind the weir,
where it fell in a waterfall into the river. The river was fast
but safe and nothing was going to keep us out of it.

The morning of New Year's Eve, the Coopers were
readying themselves to buzz off on some family expedition, leaving us to our own devices. The sun was blazing
down but the river was up. Huge torrents of water were
sweeping down it and the nearby weir had turned into a
washing machine. I'd never seen anything like it – the
power in that white water looked incredible. We had
brought a couple of boats along with us – one was a tin
canoe my father helped me build – and Alan and I were
very concerned about securing them properly in case
they got swept downstream. We pulled them up onto the
bank and left them there. Even so, we really didn't have
any idea about the brute force a river could possess.
I knew about the sea but this compressed, fast-moving
tube of water, constrained by its banks, I did not understand at all. The only thing I knew was that I was a
bloody good swimmer. I could deal with anything the
water threw at me.

Alan hopped into his parents' car and they disappeared. Dad drove us all out to the local shops where we

did a few errands, then we headed back to the river. On the way back Bronwyn and I announced that we wanted malted milkshakes, so the old man said he'd make us one when we got back to the camp.

The first thing we did when we got back was scoot down to the river and have a look at how hard it was running. There was practically a waterfall going over the top of the weir and Dad and I just looked at each other. I said, 'I bet you I could swim right over the top of that.'

He said, 'You're on.'

I saw it as another challenge, another game. So did Dad. It wasn't going to be a problem at all. The water was running fast but I had never in my life struck water I couldn't cope with. I could swim anywhere, any time, any place. So I just looked at him and said, 'Come on, then. Let's do it.'

My first go was fantastic fun: I jumped into the river, got whooshed straight over the weir, then swam the 30 metres or so back to the bank, where I pulled myself out. It felt like a huge, natural waterslide so I did the most natural thing in the world. I ran back up to where Dad was and jumped straight in to do it all again.

The second I hit the water, things went wrong. Instead of shooting straight over the weir I found myself plunged under the river and pinned down on the bottom. It held me down so long my lungs were bursting, then I shot up above the water like a champagne cork and started gulping in air, only to realise I was pinned against the weir wall. The water was turning back on itself and I couldn't break free.

The current kept pulling me under, sucking me down, nailing me to the bottom and then releasing me so I'd shoot back up to the surface, lungs screaming but nowhere nearer the river bank or anything I could grab hold of. I clocked the current, tried to swim against it and got pulled straight down again. Next thing I'm back up, gasping for breath and thinking, I'm pinned. Crank it up. Swim out. Turn on all the power.

Nothing made any difference. I just could not move a foot against the force of the water. There was nothing to grab onto. I reached out to grasp something, anything, but my fists closed on nothing, over and over, then I went under again. The next time my mouth broke water, I sucked in some air and yelled out in complete panic for the first time in my life: 'Dad, help me. Help me. Please.' I could see him on the bank and I started screaming my head off before the current pushed me back under. The next thing I felt was his hand on my arm as he grabbed me and tried to swim both of us against the current. It's over, I thought. I'm free.

Dad was very fit, a ball of muscle with no fat on him at all. He was always much faster in the water than me too. When we raced, he won, and it never crossed my mind he wouldn't be able to get me out. But he didn't have enough power either, and the second he ran out of puff and started flailing, I saw his head go under. Then the water pulled me back down too.

We both resurfaced, gasping for breath. I could see Mum, Bronwyn and Mark on the bank running and screaming at us. We were yelling: 'Get a rope, get a rope, get a rope.' Mum ran off, found one and started coming out across the top of the weir. The next thing I knew she was in the water, rope and all, but she didn't fight the river, she didn't even struggle, and when she went down, the water slammed her against the river bottom, slid her past the danger zone and popped her up beyond the white water. I saw her climb out onto the river bank and look back at us with a hideous grimace of disbelief etched into her pale, scared face.

Dad and I were getting pushed down, bobbing up, and being pushed under again at different times. There was one moment when we both came up for air together and he said, 'Where's your mother?'

I gasped, 'She's out, she's okay.'

He said, 'Okay,' and then – puff – he disappeared again. Before the water pulled me back under I thought I saw Mum running off to get help.

Other people started appearing on the bank and I knew there was a rope up there somewhere. I kept thinking, throw the bloody thing in; get us out of here. They were country people, though, they didn't have a clue how to throw a rope into water, and the next thing I knew there was an inner tube in the water. Dad and I both made a grab for it. It didn't stop us getting sucked under but when our heads were above the water and we were trying to fill our lungs again, we used it to keep ourselves up. Every time my head broke the surface I looked over at those people. They still had the rope. I had it all planned out – if somebody belts that rope around their waist, walks out onto the weir and jumps in, we can grab him and everyone else on the bank can grab the end of the rope and they could pull us out. We'd all be out of there. But no one did.

I started thinking about what you'd call today an 'exit strategy' for both of us. I could see a stump sticking out of the river and I was thinking in a very clear, calm way that if we could get to that stump we could rest and then get out. That is classic David thinking; I've been doing that ever since.

Dad was beginning to tire. Every time our heads burst up out of the water we'd lunge for the tube and hang onto it for grim death, fighting against the river until it swept us off again and pushed us back down into the turbulence. We'd go down, burst up, fight our way back to the tube, suck in some air and wait to be pummelled back under again.

Suddenly Dad's head appeared from beneath the churning water – and he was so close to me I could feel his breath. He looked me in the eye and said, 'It looks like we'll both go together, son.' He was quiet; very, very calm. It was as though he'd reached some weird acceptance of what he thought was going to happen.

I thought, bugger you, mate, the fight's not over here yet. I'm not done.

A minute later my father disappeared. He let go of the inner tube and didn't come back up. I never saw him again.

Somehow the people on the bank finally got a rope to me and dragged me out. I sat exhausted on the grassy bank, stark naked because my swimming costume had been ripped off by the river, which carried on rushing through as though nothing had happened, as though it was taunting me. Someone threw a blanket over me and I sat there shaking, thinking how stupid I was. How ridiculous. Naked, wet, exhausted and my father was gone.

I stumbled over to the tent with the others, grabbed some clothes and began pulling them on. An ambulance turned up. Mum was off her tree, crying hysterically. She understood perfectly what had happened. We kids knew it but it hadn't sunk in. I told Mum over and over again, 'It'll be alright. Don't cry. Everything's going to be fine.' Nothing was going to be alright. I got it wrong again.

We all climbed into the back of the ambulance and Mum began crying over and over, 'Don't leave me, Reg. Don't leave me. What am I going to do?' I started feeling my childhood slip away. If Dad wasn't there it was all down to me, I started thinking in complete confusion, but I wasn't in a fit state to look after myself, let alone anyone else. I sat there watching Mum being upset as the ambulance bumped and rattled us along the country roads, thinking, how can I comfort her? All the while knowing there was nothing anyone – especially me – could do.

At the hospital they wanted to check me over, I guess because I had spent a lot of time in the water, so I found myself separated from everyone again; this time by doctors, fluorescent lights and steel gurneys. Mum, Bronwyn and Mark went down one corridor while I found myself pushed down another. I was poked, prodded, made to sit down and then stand up again, all the while being asked question after question after pointless, stupid question by faceless men in spotless coats. Things started to become a blur.

There was nothing much wrong with me beyond exhaustion, so the hospital finally let me go. Once we were all back together, Mum told me I had to ring Dad's older brother Harry, and tell him what had happened. That was a very hard phone call to make. I remember thinking how unfair it was that I should have to be the person that had to do it, but I picked up the receiver and started slowly dialling the numbers, one by one. The universe shrank down until I was nothing but fingertips pushing the telephone dial around, the noise of the phone clicking its way through the exchange, the metallic ring-ringing at the other end and then my voice, which no longer belonged to me, saying, 'Uncle Harry, it's David. Something terrible has happened. Dad is dead. He's just dead.'

Back at the campsite we sat in the caravan, wait-ing – although we knew the awful truth – for a man who was never going to return. My mother's father finally drove up and we kids watched as she walked over and collapsed in his arms. We picked up a few bags and went back to my grandmother's house.

By the time the Coopers got back from their day out, Uncle Harry had made it to the campsite. He pulled Ken Cooper to one side and told him the news. As the two of them packed up the campsite and drove everything home, all Ken could think was, how could this have happened to Reg? He was so fit, so strong.

Later on, Harry and Ken came back with a boat. They spent three days driving up and down the river, scouring every nook and cranny for my father. In the end it was the police who found him, after he surfaced much further downstream than anyone expected. Harry was there and had to identify the body.

I suppose there must have been a lot of running around beforehand, but I don't remember much about the funeral at all. Uncle Harry tells me it was a small, private affair in a little wooden church in Caringbah. It was run by Fred Camroux, a family friend and priest who had been a prisoner of war in Changi and had already seen more than his fair share of tragedy. I am told that I did not react to my father's death with tears. Instead I became completely silent for so long afterwards that friends and relatives started muttering to each other about what would happen if I insisted on bottling every-thing up. I just watched and waited.

Uncle Harry had the gruesome job of putting together all the material for the official inquest. He interviewed my mother, who was an absolute mess, and me to find out exactly what had happened. He wanted to know why Dad and I were in the water and I didn't tell him about the bet. I thought for years that it was the first time in my life I ever lied, but looking back on it it wasn't really a lie, it just wasn't the absolute truth. Nothing would be served by telling him, I thought to myself. So I told him I had been playing the game that Alan and I had developed, running behind the weir to prove we could do it. Except this time, the weir wasn't just a few inches wide, it was a nightmarish running torrent. 'Dad jumped in to save me,' I said. Uncle Harry wrote it all down.

At the inquest my knees were knocking together as I stood there beside my uncle and told the officials what I thought was a lie. Things are very black and white when you're that age, and all I could think was that what I was telling them was not true. I nearly broke down and told them the real version of events, then I thought, no. It wasn't going to change anything. And maybe I needed to keep something private; to keep something of Dad back. I was furious at those people on the bank because I thought they could have saved Dad. I judged them as a fourteen-year-old does judge – completely and with no room for argument. I thought, yes, it was me who got my dad into trouble, but he would be alive today if they had done the right thing.

Uncle Harry drove my mother, grandmother and me to the inquest and when the whole horrible ordeal was over we stopped by a field to have a cup of tea from his thermos and some sandwiches he had packed for us. I had a sprained ankle at the time, so I was on crutches – like I said, I always had some injury or other – and as I hobbled into the grass to eat my sandwich I spotted the biggest snake I had ever seen in my life sitting motionless there, all coiled up in the summer sun. God, he was a big bastard, a huge old brown snake. He just stared at me with his cold, unblinking, reptile eyes. Blaming me. I backed away slowly and said to Uncle Harry, 'Let's get out of here. I want to go home.'

One other thing happened that day. After Harry dropped us back home, I stopped being subservient. Up until then, people had called me a dickhead and I'd agreed with them. I had let it slide. After this, if someone called me a dickhead, they got sorted. When the new year began, I went back to school with all the other kids. It hadn't changed, but I had. I started talking back, even hitting back. I got into shouting matches with teachers and fist-fights with other pupils.

The previous year, the school authorities had moved me to class 1J, a 'general activities' class. These were the classes for the hopeless kids who had made their way to the bottom of the school barrel. There were constant disruptions – arguments breaking out and chairs being thrown around. This was a tough bunch of kids. We'd all been through the mill, we all pretty much thought school was a waste of time, and we were totally uninterested.

The first schoolteacher to tackle this turmoil had been an old man – Pop Clay, we called him. He was ninety in the shade and about as round as he was tall. He walked into 1J and put his hands down his pants. 'Oh no,' someone said, 'he's going to have a wank.' But no, he whipped out this cane from his trouser leg and whacked it down on the desk. One of the kids walked up, took it off him, broke it in half and threw it out the window. Pop Clay was lucky he didn't get thrown out of the window as well.

Two-thirds of the way through the year he disappeared and Mr Jeffries turned up. He was the weirdest character I had ever seen in my life. He had Marty

Feldman pop-eyes, glasses, and wore his belt up over the top of his rotund belly, so he looked pregnant. To cap it all, he always insisted on wearing a long grey dustcoat.

When he appeared, everyone in 1J burst out laughing. He called the room to order, picked half a dozen of the kids, gave them some money and sent them off to buy newspapers. Then he would sit us down in groups and get us to find things – sporting results, the first horse in the last race, the politicians' row of the day. The newspapers became our textbooks. We'd go through them and talk about what we found there. I learnt more about life and the way the world worked in those groups of four or five than I'd ever dreamt of before. I discovered current affairs, history, mathematics, how the stockmarket makes the world go round.

Mr Jeffries had real belief that the kids in his care could learn, even if they couldn't read. For the first time in a schoolroom I was excited and stimulated. Suddenly learning seemed relevant and I wanted to know more. 'Why are the Chinese trying to get into the United Nations?' I asked him one day. 'And why are the Americans trying to stop them?' My teacher actually sat and talked to me about it – the first time a teacher had ever done that. We discussed why laws are fought for, what the effect of religion can be.

In this class of supposedly the stupidest, most troublesome children in the school, conversation would sparkle around the sophisticated nuances of interactions and circumstances. He gave us – me – the credit of being able to grasp those ideas. Mr Jeffries was the first person, apart from my father, that I really felt respected me. Then my father died. Mr Jeffries stayed with my class, now 2J, and he did his best. But it was all too little, too late. There was no way I could complete my academic year, so in July I found a job at a cabinet-maker's, and at fourteen-and-a-half I was granted a special exemption to leave, exiting the school system much as I had entered it nine years earlier: illiterate and basically uneducated. My childhood was over.

4

THE SEASONS MOVED ON that year without me. Deep inside I had frozen completely. As though it was the most natural thing in the world, twelve months after my father's death it was somehow summer again, one of those long, languid height-of-holiday afternoons when the hours melt into eternities and all you can think about is cooling down. Christmas weather. The kind that brings surprises. Mum must have known there was going to be trouble. She primed me with the words: 'By the way, dear, a friend of mine has brought his boat up the top driveway. It's a speedboat and he wants to take us water-skiing. What do you think of that, then?'

Now, you had to do a lot wrong to lose me if you owned a speedboat. I thought they were very cool indeed; the one vessel our family never possessed. I had a sailing boat, a VJ in which I was learning to master the winds all too slowly, but we did our family boating in two vessels – a skiff, and a big 18-foot motorboat with an inboard motor that was way too big for me to handle and was now gathering dust below the house. That had been my father's boat. Before he died we had all spent a lot of time in that boat, going for picnics and roaming around the waterways. We had grown up with it; it was part of all our lives. So at the words 'friend' and 'speedboat', I sprinted up the drive – to see the boat, not the bloke – and was disappointed to spot a rather small vessel, one my father and I would have called a runabout, with an outboard motor. It was a far cry from the huge, powerful machine that had punched its way into my fifteen-year-old imagination.

'David, this is my friend Rex,' said Mum, hot on my heels.

A tall, very upright man held a sturdy hand out for me to shake and, as he did so, a wave of white uniforms, drills and antiseptic washed over me. Good grief, it was my dentist.

My mother was trying to sound casual and started chatting away to her new friend about the weather and the conditions on the bay, but something inside me piped up. Friend of yours? Male? What is going on here? Dad's death was twelve months behind us but his ghost walked with me every single day. As my mother twittered about in the blinding heat, trying to make everyone feel at home, Dad's spectre stood behind my shoulder watching Rex's every move. The poor man did not stand a chance.

Rex and I launched his 'powerboat' at a nearby ramp

and threw the water-skiing equipment into the back, ready to motor out into the bay. Rex put the key into the engine and turned it. Great, his boat wouldn't start. Then it wasn't powerful enough to keep me above the water during a series of doomed attempts at water-skiing. I was a big, heavy lad and all Rex's efforts to get some power out of his boat came to nothing. Instead of the great day's water-skiing that he and my mother had planned to sweeten me into a friendship with the man, I found myself angry and frustrated, and very busy scrutinising the pair of them, hypersensitised to any clue that something untoward was going on.

In one way the pairing made perfect sense. Sure, Rex Booth was our dentist – he had been pulling our family's teeth for decades – but he was also a widower, with a background almost as tragic as our own. Lorna, his former wife, had died two years earlier after four devastatingly difficult years of battling Hodgkin's disease. The couple's three children were traumatised by their mother's long illness and desperate for some kind of settled life. They had discovered Lorna was sick while she was still pregnant with the youngest Booth child, Paul, so his earliest years were spent being shuttled between his mother when she had the strength to cope with him, and anybody else who would step into the breach.

Rex and my mother should have been a perfect match – widow and widower joining forces Brady Bunch style to create one big, happy household. Well, guess what? That meant nothing to me. All I knew was that someone was muscling in on my father's territory. As Rex revved up his so-called powerboat's engine to get the three of us back to shore, I shouldered past him and plonked myself down between where he was about to sit, and my mother, so the pair of them could not touch each other. I glared at him all the way home.

I would love to say that I came to my senses after that but in truth it was downhill all the way from there. Mum refused to take any nonsense from me. Ignoring my best efforts to poison her against this evil interloper, she gradually introduced my siblings and me to Rex's family – Robyn, who at ten was three years younger than Bronwyn; Alan, the same age as our brother Mark, and, of course, Paul, the baby of the bunch. My introduction to Paul, who was ten years my junior, came in the form of a helpless squeal emanating from the vicinity of our toilet. 'Go and get him, David,' someone yelled, so off I trotted, pushing open the door to see this kid, bent over the toilet seat, bum up, waiting for it to be wiped. I do love reminding him of that.

The fact that I remember that incident is an exception. Rex's children were virtually irrelevant to me back then, and I refused to let any of them come anywhere near the brittle emotional barracks I had built around myself. I was fifteen, and full of fury and ego. All I cared about was getting rid of Rex. The last happy memories I had of my father were of the pair of us sitting beneath our home's front balcony, building a boat together. A boat that was meant for me. Then – bang. He is not there, the house is empty, and my dentist is muscling in. As I saw things, Rex had no idea how to build a boat, let alone a family. And he certainly did not know how to handle me.

Summer melted into the calm winds of autumn; then winter came. Rex was still in the picture. As he and my mother wanted to knit their lives together, he became very concerned about me. Unfortunately, his solution was to suggest that I undergo some private schooling. He felt that throwing more education my way would sort things out. I was too far gone for that by then. So I railed at every suggestion he made and took things out on my exhausted mother, who copped it every which way to Christmas. Her priority was keeping the family clothed and fed after my father's death, and she spent every spare hour working as a typist–clerk to put food on our table. She needed all the help she could get at home. So what did I do? I refused point-blank to do anything around the house. I was uncooperative, argumentative and in a constant state of readiness for the next battle, which I fought as if my life depended on it, even if it was only about something like why I had refused, yet again, to do the washing up. On matters of minor importance, I would declare that black was white for no good reason until I was blue in the face. When I had something serious to say, I became vicious with fury.

'He is not my father!' I would scream at her, after she had brought me a cup of coffee or put a hot evening meal in front of me. 'What is he doing here? Get him out of this house. What is wrong with you?'

One night as we were all eating together and I was busy doing my usual thing of arguing about absolutely everything, Rex secretly turned a tape machine on and started recording me. After a few minutes, he stopped my rant in mid-flow and played it back to me with the words: 'Listen to yourself. See what you sound like.'

Bad move. He thought it would help. All he did was put me on the spot, and I exploded.

The more friends that Rex introduced my mother to, the more nails I tried to hammer into his coffin, managing only to bury myself ever more deeply. I could not see that she was trying to move on with her life. Instead, I interpreted her efforts to get to know Rex's social circle as her turning her back on her old friends, which I took as another rejection of my father. So I shouted and screamed about that as well.

The two men had enormously different personalities, which probably did not help matters either. Rex's values and attitudes were poles apart from what I was used to, and he didn't share my father's easy comfort with strangers. While Dad spent his spare time helping friends and workmates, Rex kept his attention much closer to home. More seriously for my mother, my father had loved the cut and thrust of a good verbal stoush. He would argue his case with relish until the cows came home. Rex, on the other hand, was a quiet, highly focused and determined man who could not stand arguments. 'You and Rex could never live together,' my mother told me one night after I had outdone myself shouting, yet again. I knew she was right and felt bathed in a thin satisfaction.

My triumph proved to be short-lived. There were five

other children to consider as well as me, all of them younger and still at school. So my mother moved into Rex's house in Caringbah, and left me alone in what had been the Pescud family home. At first it was fantastic; the pain and problems seemed to pack up and walk out the moment the rest of my family did. All that remained was me and the shell of our life, and the deep, dark water below.

Every morning I got myself up and trudged off to work at a joinery shop, where I was beginning to learn the basics of carpentry, a trade that turned out to be very useful as the years progressed. I lasted six months in that job before they threw me out for laziness and insubordination; a minor setback, as it turned out. I would prove to be unusually good at convincing people who had never met me before to give me jobs.

Before long I moved in with my grandparents, who were more than happy to try and get me on the straight and narrow. Then came the bombshell: Rex and my mother had got married. Mum was so afraid of our reactions that she had been unable to bring herself to tell any of us what they had planned. She and Rex disappeared one day and tied the knot in private, with only my aunt and Rex's sister as witnesses. Her guilt about me was consuming her but she stuck to her guns and refused to let me sabotage what she felt was a last stab at happiness.

Once married, the troubled couple persuaded various relatives to look after their children while they went on a honeymoon – which, in classic Rex style, involved flitting from one dental convention to another in a three-month round-the-world trip that took them to Hawaii, San Francisco, New York and Vienna. It was the first time my mother had been abroad – the first time she had been anywhere, really – and she did enjoy the trip. But at the back of her mind she could not quiet her worries about how her children were managing without her.

When she and Rex came back, they rented out our old family home and then invited everyone to move into the house they had had built in Caringbah. Everyone, that is, except me. Mum remembers telling me straight: 'David, I don't think you can come and live with us. It would never work, you know that as well as I do. We just cannot all live together.'

I have no recollection of that at all. All I know is that I alone did not get invited to move in. I could not believe it. There was no way I was going to live in the same house as Rex, but how dare my mother deny me the right to turn her down. I felt as though I was being thrown out of everybody's lives. My mother's logic was clear, if horribly painful. As she would later explain, she was well aware that her children were suffering. Even so, she would say, 'If I had turned Rex down I might not have had another chance to marry again. The younger boys had a great time, they stepped into a ready-made family of their own age. Robyn came around not long after we wed, but Bronwyn and David had terrible trouble with it. Rex and I wrestled with our consciences, but what could we do?' The guilt was enormous but she could not see any other way. 'There were five other children to look out for and there was no way David and Rex could live together, it would have been the end of us,' she would tell people. So that was that.

My mother says she told me it was all for the best and that she would make sure I always had somewhere to live. However sugar-coated she made it, the message was clear. I was on my own. Where there should have been six kids, a kind of shell-shocked Brady Bunch, there were only five. I was out; all the other children were in. David Pescud the fuckwit had struck again.

Before long my grandmother let it be known that she could no longer cope with the miserable, obstreperous character I had become. My grandfather was suffering from high blood pressure, and he could no longer handle my continual bickering, so my mother organised for me to live in a boarding house in Cronulla. I left in a deep, dark fury. During the years that followed, my family and I made the odd stab at reconciliation, which invariably collapsed in a heap. I was lonely and I did want a family but every time I tried to rejoin my own, it seemed to end up in yet another fight.

I started pinning my hopes on my girlfriend. Yes, I actually had a girlfriend. And what a girlfriend she was: smart, pretty, astute, capable and utterly trustworthy. At sixteen, Margaret Whitehead was what everyone I had met so far aspired to be. I told her pretty early on that I was illiterate, and no sooner were the words out of my mouth than I had an ally. One of the things about disabilities is that you always feel very alone. You are isolated, separate, different. When I told Margaret, in my stumbling way, 'I can't read or write,' it did not bother her a bit. She refused to judge me, instead automatically starting to help me, and because of that she didn't scare me. I really trusted her.

So we went out, had fun, and made out, like normal kids that age do. Finally, I thought, this is how a real person should feel. It was hardly any surprise then, that I blurted out the ultimate question one night on her parents' quiet front porch, after we had been out to the pictures and I had walked her back home.

'Margaret, will you marry me?'

'Don't be stupid,' came the reply. She always was a very sensible girl.

'Oh. Right. Goodnight then. See you Tuesday, yeah?'

'Yes. See you then.'

Off I trotted into the dark, having failed once more. Nice one, Pescud, I thought to myself. You can't even do that right.

Behind the scenes, my mother was trying to help me out where she could. Rex's brother-in-law had a factory that churned out steel furniture. They were in need of cheap labour and offered me a job, and some months later an apprenticeship in fitting and machining. Amazingly, I hung on to it for two years, passing all my practical exams but failing all the theory tests. Of course. I was not even capable of reading the questions, let alone answering them on paper.

The head teacher at the college where the classes and tests took place could not understand what was happening. 'What is going on?' he asked me one lunchtime.

'I had you pegged to be a good apprentice. You seem bright. You have a very good memory. And you are doing good work. What's the problem with the theory exams?'

'I don't understand the questions,' I mumbled back. 'I can't really, um, get to grips with them.'

'Look, there's somebody from St George TAFE I want you to see.'

'Right,' I said, listening to his directions and trotting off. Whatever. Here we go again.

Up until then every 'expert' I had been to had thought that I must have had an eye problem. I had done a lot of looking through lenses, and answering questions about my eyesight while opticians tried to work out where my problem lay. So I walked into this specialist's office, sat down opposite his big desk and waited for him to get his optical equipment out. Instead he started asking me a series of rather stupid questions along the lines of:

'You are out in the middle of the bush, you're lost. Which way is north?

'You get in a car, the engine won't turn over; something is broken. What do you do?

'A man lives on the tenth floor of a building. Every day he takes the elevator to go down to the ground floor to go to work or to go shopping. When he returns he takes the elevator to the seventh floor and walks up the stairs to reach his apartment on the tenth floor. He hates walking, so why does he do it?

'A man walks into a bar and asks the barman for a glass of water. The barman pulls out a gun and points it at the man. The man says, "Thank you," and walks out. Why?'

Quiz over, he produced some big pieces of card with weird blotches of black ink splattered all over them. 'What does this look like?' he asked me, handing me the first card. I gazed down at the misshapen blob.

'It looks like an ink spot to me. What does it look like to you?'

'Fair enough,' he said, with a laugh.

After what felt like several hours of intense questioning, he finally came out with it. 'Do you know what you've been doing here?' Of course, the answer was no.

'I have just given you an IQ test, among other things.'

'Oh. What's that then?'

He told me.

'Right, I see.' There was no way I was going to ask him how I had done.

'Look, kid,' the man said, 'there is absolutely nothing wrong with your intelligence. You have a rather high IQ. So, well done. That's just great.'

'Why can't I read then?'

'Because you have dyslexia.'

It was a Wednesday afternoon, one of those sharp, cold days in July, and I can still smell the wax on his polished office floor. He kept talking at me, trying to explain what my condition was, what it meant, how much was understood and what he could do to help – yet more reading classes, apparently. Wonderful. I couldn't take much of it in but when I finally stood up and shook the specialist's hand, everything seemed to have shifted sideways. I had an answer but it did not make sense.

It would be years before I told anybody about the diagnosis. Virtually everyone I had ever met had told me I was stupid, and I was afraid that if I threw the word 'dyslexia' at them, they would just say: 'Bullshit, you *are* a dickhead, Pescud.' So I kept it to myself.

The specialist booked me in for yet more classes in a futile attempt to get me reading. The only difference between what I sat through then and the classes I had gone through before was that me and all of the other pupils were even older. We were still a bunch of losers, as far as I could see. I stuck the classes out for a while, then left, with very little achieved.

Outside work, my home life continued to disintegrate, largely because I did not have a home. Before long I was bouncing around cheap flats in the shire to keep clear of Rex and my new family. I owed landladies and landlords money, I had jobs but never much cash, so I would wait until my rent was due and then duck it by doing a runner. It was around that time that I first slept on the streets.

Some new friends lived in a squat in what was then Sydney's seediest suburb, Kings Cross, a place that looked like fairyland to me, so I crashed with them when I could, which was not that often. When the squat was off-limits, I would spend my nights wandering around from snooker room to card house to cabaret joints, such as the infamous Les Girls. Night after night I would find a tunnel or pull myself under a hedge, and curl up until daybreak. One of my favourite haunts, a rambling, smoky, red-daubed snooker room in Ultimo, had the added advantage of possessing a quiet set of stairs around the back, so as soon as I had frittered away what money I had, I would crash there for a few hours until the trains started up again in the morning.

It took me a while to work out which platform to go from – well, I couldn't read the signs, could I? – but I worked out how to jump the ticket barriers, dodge any inspectors who might be lurking about and scam my way onto the first train headed back to the shire in time for whatever menial job I was somehow managing to hold down. I knew that I could talk people into hiring me – I had more front than David Jones – and I used that skill with a vengeance. That did not mean I could keep the job. I would talk my way into a position in the morning, only to be told never to bother coming back by the afternoon. That year I ended up with sixteen group certificates.

Away from work, I was tooling around the edge of delinquency and discovering the joys of gangs. Some of my 'mates' were harmless enough – I ran into my old sailing buddies every now and again and would have the odd drink with them, but I was fast losing my links to the water. The musos were more of a favourite. These guys were very cool because they were all in a band. I had a bass guitar which I couldn't play to save my life, but they let me hang out with them anyway.

Then there were the rev-headed petrol guys. That mob were trouble. We used to break into cars – a ridiculously easy process if you had a coathanger and rudimentary knowledge of how to jump-start engines – and all pile in for a joyride. We dumped our new wheels when we got bored with them, usually after about an hour's drive or so, taking a childish delight in never leaving them anywhere that their pissed-off owners would be likely to find them.

Fuelling into the heady mix of alcohol and teenage sex came a new craving: violence. Deep inside me lay not plain anger but a red-hot, lava-like fury ready to erupt at any moment. I would become so infuriated that all I wanted to do was smash things up – very annoying, given that I also had a huge aversion to damaging other people's property. So I never went about trashing phone boxes. Breaking into corner stores and letting rip with a baseball bat and a tin of paint was definitely not my style. Oh no. I went for people.

One of my specialities was starting fights. Walking down the road, if a passer-by so much as glanced at me the wrong way, I would punch them in the stomach. Anybody who brushed past me or said something within my earshot that I assumed was about me, whether it was or not, would feel my fists. I used to do karate classes with a mate once a week. One time I was driving us home down the main street of Caringbah when we spotted some girls getting off the train on one side of the street. Parked on the other was a big black 21 Division Rambler, the cop car of choice. So we did what any good hoons in a hotted-up FJ Holden would do: a big wheelie, a roar up to the Rambler and a torrent of catcalls at the girls.

Before I could say 'Oh bugger', the cops were pulling me out of the car and taking the piss out of my karate uniform. No, I hadn't bothered getting changed after karate. I saw red and started giving as good as I got – Lord knows why, because this guy was six foot six and built like a toilet block. The next thing I know, I'm face-down in the gutter with his boot in my neck. Why he didn't arrest me, I have no idea. I suppose I was not worth the trouble.

Another evening that sticks in my mind, I got into a fight with a stranger which he started – a very unusual event. He called me some name for no reason that I could see, so I pushed him into an alley and got stuck in big time. Pinning the guy against a wall with one hand, I tore into him, slamming blow after kidney-crunching blow into his buckling torso, over and over again, refusing to let him go down. Without warning, the raging torrent inside of me switched itself off. I let him fall, turned around and walked away, leaving the guy bleeding and rasping to catch his breath in a bone-blistered heap on the filthy alley floor.

Behind my ready fists, the uncertainties kept swirling. Thoughts of despair and hopelessness regularly crowded their way into my brain, usually in the afternoons once I had knocked off work. Perhaps I was lonely; going 'home' did not really mean anything to me any more. There was no one to go home to anyway.

My one port in the storm was Aunt Betty, my mother's younger sister, who is long dead now. When I needed a meal and someone to talk to I would head around to her home in Kirrawee, where this lovely, soft woman with a smile like a hot cup of soup on a cold day would welcome me with open arms.

She let me rant, rave and vent some of the truckload of steam that was building up inside of me. Betty did not judge, she just put on the coffee, pulled out the biscuits and let me talk for as long as I needed to. When I'd worn myself out, she would pat me on the head and put me up for the night. She was a life raft, no doubt about it, but I was being torn apart by a stronger force than Betty, and as the jobs I found myself in came and went, everything seemed increasingly pointless. I walked so close to suicide so many times, standing on the top of tall buildings, willing myself to jump. But killing myself involved settling on a method and diving into concrete from a great height was not really me. The answer, when it popped into my tortured adolescent head, seemed obvious. The water.

So one chilly Friday afternoon after work I trotted off to Cronulla, stripped to my bathers – I always wore Speedos for undies in those days – and started swimming east. There was not much of a plan. I would swim out to sea and just keep on going. Then, if I changed my mind, I would not be able to get back.

I stroked my way out through what felt like a warm, velvet ocean for what must have been hours, because when I turned around and took what was supposed to be my final look at the shore, it was several miles away. I had gone over the horizon and could not see the beach. I was tiring, so I rolled over and turned around, thinking, right, I'll swim back and drown on the way in. It is a long, long way and I'll never make it.

Wrong, wrong, wrong. I had swum a lot in my life and I was a strong, 12-stone survival machine. I knew how not to drown. Halfway back in to land, as it became gut-wrenchingly clear that tonight was not the night, I rolled over onto my back, watched the city lights twinkling in the distance and thought, you idiot, you can't even kill yourself properly. Then I just floated in the water, gazing at the stars. I'll wait a while until I get my breath, then I'll head in, I thought. I must have been exhausted because I remember a kind of languid euphoria sweeping over me as a couple of waves picked me up and carried me back in to the beach.

It was pitch-black by the time I hit dry land, around nine or ten o'clock at night. I sat on the sand wondering, what can I do to stop feeling like this? I thought it through. I could not stop the waves of despair that continued to engulf me, but I did not really want to die. That was clear. What I did want was to make the people who were supposed to care for me hurt. Why wouldn't they listen to me? Couldn't they see what I was going through? As ever, the answer seemed to be the water. Water was the safe place. It was also the place that killed my dad. It was the place I loved. Even then, I knew it was where I belonged. But it did not want to claim me that day.

So I drank and fought my way through the weekend that followed and, come Monday, went back to work; to the early mornings, the ever-blackening afternoons, the long, violent evenings. To the fractured life that passed for a whole.

Every now and again I would get a whiff of the waxy polish I smelt on that specialist's floor, and remember the diagnosis I had been given by the first person I had ever met who had seen me for what I was. Not an idiot, incapable of learning, but a young man with a nameable, quantifiable condition. A door was kicked open that day. It took me decades to pluck up the courage to walk through it, but as I left the specialist's office and walked slowly down the pristine, waxy corridor out into the harsh winter sunlight beyond, everything had changed.

I wasn't stupid any more, I was dyslexic. Big difference.

5

IT WAS 1966, and things were rocking. The miniskirt was in, the Beatles were more famous than Jesus and I was in trouble. I never found out exactly who dobbed me in, which was probably just as well given my state of mind at the time, but things came to a head at 5 am one morning as I was torn from semi-consciousness by two big, burly police officers in full uniform and curled lip.

The scene was Flyde Street, Caringbah – Mrs Mac's house – a neat, freshly painted four-bedroom fibro boasting the landlady from heaven. She had come to the outskirts of Sydney from the country years before with her son, and she vaguely knew my family. Mrs Mac, with an absent husband and an ageing mother, needed to top up her earnings by putting boarders in her two spare bedrooms, one in the house, the other in a makeshift cut-off at the end of the verandah. That is where I stayed.

Being on the edge of the house had the added advantage that I could sneak in and out without disturbing anyone too much. Until that morning.

The first I knew was when someone grabbed me by the shoulder and shook me until I opened my eyes to see the two officers of the law and the tiny head of my landlady with a furious frown burnt into her livid little face. Hey, man, this is a bit out there, I remember thinking as I grabbed at consciousness. I came to and realised – oh bugger – I was completely naked. So I did what any self-respecting, fully grown nineteen-year-old would have done. I pulled the bedsheets up to my chin and started yelling at the coppers: 'Get out! I haven't got any clothes on! Fuck you, I'm going to punch your fucking lights out if you don't get out!'

Well, they didn't get out and I didn't punch their lights out either. The two of them stood their ground, towering over me in my tiny, dingy room, with their arms folded in a very unimpressed fashion. I suffered the indignity of their glares while I scrabbled around on the floor to find my undies and as soon as I'd pulled them on, the questions began.

'Look, mate, we haven't got all morning. We know what you've been up to, what we want now is the gear. Where have you stashed it? Where is the "hot stuff"?'

Oh no. *That*'s what this was all about.

I had recently driven back in my hotted-up FJ Holden from a job in the Snowy Mountains. I spent months working on that car, replacing everything that looked the least bit rusty or was running out of steam, and buffing the bodywork until it gleamed as proudly as I did. On the scrounge for cash, I then decided to sell some of the spare parts I had been cannibalising and no longer needed, and I spent a day chasing round auto-part shops in an attempt to flog my manifolds and twin carburettors, mouthing off ten to the dozen to anyone interested in second-hand car parts about what I had. I used the term 'hot stuff' rather a lot.

It turned out that the night before I appeared on the scene, someone had broken into a shop and stolen a pile of gear remarkably similar to the stuff I was trying to unload, so the cops put out an all-points alert, some shop owner put two and two together and took the number plate of my car and next thing you know, it's five in the morning, the police are breathing down my naked neck and Mrs Mac is having kittens because there's a cop car outside her nice respectable house and she can feel the curtains twitching all the way down her street.

That is my story and I'm sticking to it.

My bedroom was tiny; the dresser was jammed up against the foot of my single bed. There were shelves against the only free wall and boxes all over the floor. I started pulling all my spare car parts out from under the bed, twin manifolds, exhausts – you name it, I had it stashed under there. 'No,' said the taller officer, taking a quick look. 'The other stuff. The "hot stuff".'

'But that's it,' I said.

They didn't believe a word of it and started turning over my room, pulling out my drawers and tipping them upside down. Every box was emptied, every carton turned on its tail.

'Put my pyjamas back, mate,' I heard myself moaning with pathetic impotence as foul-smelling socks, towels, LPs and a mound of washing that would have been better off in an incinerator started piling up in the middle of the room.

'Oh God, leave those magazines alone.' Nup, there they were, out of their hiding place in all their X-rated glory. I stole a glance at Mrs Mac, whose scowl deepened into an even blacker shade of thunder. As an illiterate I did not even have the excuse that I was only buying them for the articles. Bugger. Her beady eyes bored into me more deeply.

My heart was hammering. Not because I had stolen car parts hidden away in some crevice the cops were about to stick their fat fingers into. Oh no. What I knew and they had yet to discover was that I had a drug stash hidden away in that room. Nothing major, you understand. Just a bit for my own personal use. As they pounded their way through my things, getting closer and closer to the drugs, the taller of the two suddenly decided he had had enough.

'Come on, mate, this is getting boring. What have you done with the stolen stuff?'

'I'm telling you, there isn't any.' By now I was whining.

'Fine,' came the reply. 'You won't mind if we have a look in your car then.'

Shit. I was toast. The first thing they found, tucked away under a blanket in the boot of the Holden, was a revolver. It was beautiful thing, a family heirloom dating back to around 1880 and worth a bundle. My great-grandfather first owned it and it had gradually trickled its way through my family and down to me. But the cops did not see an antique. They saw a gun and, one question later, an indictable offence. So that was that. I got arrested for possessing an unlicensed concealable firearm and was frogmarched off to the police car.

Which is really strange, looking back on things, because most other days there would have been an unlicensed 350 Magnum or a 44 or any number of navy Colts lying around. Unbeknown to Mrs Mac, I was mad about guns. I used to spend a lot of time in a gun shop in Blakehurst. My trade was machining and tool-making, which is aligned to gunsmithing, and I would help out in the machining, sometimes bedding the barrels and stocks together. The technical side of their construction – a clockwork-tight combination of timber and metal – fascinated me, as did the military connection. My generation was fed on army, navy and air force stories. Most of our fathers had come back from World War II victorious, and I suppose right and might were all connected in my mind with guns. The crew I hung around with seemed to have hundreds of weapons. They were like stamps, just a hobby, and I would develop a large collection of Winchesters and European shotguns as time went by.

I built quite a few guns, rifles mostly, and would learn to customise other people's so that they could fire more bullets than they had originally been designed to do, or hit targets at a greater range. I have always admired those who can build at a high level of craft and excellence. In those days guns – handguns, rifles, shotguns, whatever – were the epitome for me of all those things. But guns are also things you threaten and kill people with. I can honestly say that I never thought about them like that. I used to hunt a lot but I never needed a gun to protect myself. I never needed a gun to make me feel strong, and I certainly never needed a weapon to intimidate someone. Why would I? If I wanted someone to feel threatened, I could do a real good job without a gun. They did have their drawbacks too. I loaded a revolver one night when the darkness started biting into me particularly badly, and I wanted to demolish the feeling of being split in the middle. I did not have the guts to pull the trigger though.

So the back story to that police search was that I enjoyed building, rescaling and remodelling guns, as well as buying and selling them on the black market. There just didn't happen to be any in my car, or my room, that particular morning. By rights the antique revolver shouldn't have been there either, except that I'd taken it to the Snowy Mountains because it was valuable and I didn't want to leave it in my room. Like a dolt, I had then completely forgotten to stow it out of harm's way.

Mrs Mac was furious. Not only was she going to have to spend the rest of the week explaining to the neighbours what the police were doing raiding her house at the crack of sparrow's fart, but one of her lodgers had been found in possession of a firearm. She would have had a fit if she had known what I was really up to. Not that what she had to endure wasn't bad enough. The cops let me put my clothes on – gee, thanks, guys – then they snapped on a pair of handcuffs and, in full view of the early morning curtain-twitchers, 'escorted' me down my landlady's drive and unceremoniously jammed me into the police car.

Getting fingerprinted brought the whole gruesome situation home. Christ, I really had been arrested. Not only was I in trouble but I could not wipe that blue ink off my fingers. They charged me and took a statement, which they then had to read out to me. The heavy cell door clanged shut, leaving me with a tiny half-round of a window liberating nothing more than a brick view outside. I wanted my phone call now, please. And who did I ring? The only person I could think of. My mother. She turned up about four hours later and bailed me out.

When the case finally came to court I turned up in my best dark blue corduroy flared suit, which I usually wore with a strong blue shirt, a silver paisley tie and high-heeled Beatle boots. Add the sunnies and I was a cool dude, alright. My case was adjourned initially, possibly because my suit was so loud the judge couldn't hear himself think, although I seem to recall there being some legal reason as well. By the time I was called back in several months later, I had the family solicitor on my side. He argued that because of the size of the gun – the thing was a goddam cannon – no conviction should be recorded.

The judge swallowed it. Perhaps a last-minute decision to tone down my tie had impressed on him that I was capable of better things. He still put me on a five-year good behaviour bond, which shook me up a little.

After things calmed down a bit I applied for a licence for the revolver and they gave it back. I kept it at my mother's place after that, until I got married, then I had it at mine. It was a pain, though. The licence ran out every year and it had to be kept in a safe, secure place which the police came and inspected. The gun had been in the family for generations but I wasn't prepared to have the cops in and out of my home all the time, so eventually I traded it for another antique, a vintage German rifle of about the same period.

As the sixties rocked on, I struggled with the feelings churning around inside of me. Dyslexia was a sidebar to my life. I had no idea why I felt this way or what I could do about it. The cycle continued: the blackness creeping slowly towards me, until I did something – one of my virtual suicide attempts – and the gesture flushed it away.

I looked the part, usually running around in jeans and, when it was cold, a long brown duffle coat with sleeves covered in badges, including the obligatory peace insignias, Save the World pins and Vietnam protest state-ments. My hair was long and frizzy, in a salt-matted, blond afro that had me dubbed Shirley Temple, and on the outside I was all pacifism and free love. I would greet people with the hippy-dippy words: 'Peace, brother.' If they didn't say 'Peace, brother' back, I did not mess around. I just punched their lights out.

I have absolutely no recollection of 64-year-old English yachtsman Francis Chichester sailing the *Gypsy Moth IV* into Sydney in 1966, on the first leg of a journey that had him lauded as the first person to sail solo around the world – a memory blackout that amazes me today. I do remember having an extreme love of pantyhose, because pantyhose meant girls wore miniskirts. I also have almost total recall of my first LSD trip. It was a Friday, after I picked a mate of mine up and took him back through the bucketing rain to his flat. 'I know what I wanna do,' he said. 'Yeah, so do I,' I replied, and we cranked the stereo up, dropped a couple of pills and sat like zombies listening to the Rolling Stones and gazing at the changing tones of his leadlight window for hours.

Margaret and I kept going out, off and on. Work became more stable – I moved from a job as a toolmaker at an engineering factory to one as a fitter and turner. Even so, despair was never far behind.

Margaret had no interest in sailing, so it dropped right out of my life. There was no way I could stay away from the water, though, and I took up competitive diving and spear-fishing, which turned into a powerful passion. Diving became my escape. I would tear down to the water after work with my spear gun and wetsuit, winter or summer regardless. I lived for my time in the water – slipping in felt like coming home, whether I was competing against other divers to bring up the biggest fish or just taking huge lungfuls and turning over the bottom of the Harbour floor beneath ferry stops, looking for all-too-easy-to-find gold jewellery that had slipped off inadvertent fingers and necks as commuters waited for their early morning rides.

Seeing sharks in the water was not unusual. Grey nurses would glide through their territory with a fast, powerful ease I learnt to respect. They would never bother humans unless the human bothered them first. I wish I had known that when I was younger. But I did get a shock one day when I felt a sudden, severe crush on one of my legs and looked down to see a three-foot shark with its mouth wrapped around my knee. It was winter, so I was wearing a long wetsuit with a pair of wetsuit shorts over the top to protect myself against the freezing water, and my little attacker was having serious trouble sinking his teeth through all the layers of neoprene rubber. I pulled my underwater gun, an object called a Powerhead, out of my shorts and shot him through the head. When I got out of the water and pulled my wetsuits off, I found a ring of puncture marks around my leg where his teeth had made it through my skin. It hurt like buggery for a few days, but I felt sorry for the poor creature. I was probably swimming around in his hole and he was just acting territorially, so I did not think twice about the potential danger of shark attacks.

Some months later, I was forced to reassess. I was diving with a mate, Larry. We used to go down the coast south of Sydney rock-hopping, which involves jumping off rocks into deep ocean holes to find our prey. One Friday we headed down to a great secluded spot we knew about, pitched our tent and crashed.

The following morning, Larry had developed sinus problems which meant he could not dive. 'No problem,' I said. 'I'll go on my own.' Off I went, taking lungfuls of air and diving down into the depths. I could dive to about 40 feet by then, without an air tank. The water was clear and there were a lot of fish swimming around in the warm, late spring water. By the morning's end, I had speared quite a few.

In those days, before we had float lines, we had sugarbags tied about our waists, coarsely woven hessian bags about half the size of a wheat bag secured onto our belts. The trick was to shoot the fish, pull it in, pop it in the bag and carry on. A good system, but it did mean that the diver was trailing a line of fresh blood from the thickest part of his body. Later on we moved to six-foot float lines and more sophisticated methods, but this was way back.

I had been pulling loads of fish out of the sea, including a couple of very tasty-looking crayfish. Every time my sugarbag was full, I swam back in towards the rocks and handed my catch over to Larry, who would give me another bag before starting the messy job of cleaning them and stowing them away in an Esky so we could take home a good haul for friends and family. It was hard work and we carried on all day.

At about four in the afternoon I went down for my last dive from an isthmus Larry and I walked out to through waist-deep water. The isthmus had some gutters that ran parallel south-east of it and were full of jewfish. I had been going back to one particular spot all day looking for them but had not caught sight of any of the little buggers. Larry wanted me to shoot him some gropers before we finished – spear-fishing gropers was legal back then – and I wanted to go back to the gutters and also check a hole where I thought there might be a few more crayfish. So I swam back out and came in behind the isthmus in about 20 feet of water. I ducked and dived up and down, looking for brown gropers, and suddenly I spotted one, about 18 inches long, a nice five or six pounder. Bang, I speared him.

Coming back up to the surface I glimpsed a shadow out of the corner of my eye. Spending a lot of time under the water makes you very aware of your environment. When the waves start moving in a different direction you know it and wonder what is going on. As that shadow flew past I thought, uh-oh.

Up at the surface I trod water with my flippers and pulled in my spear. I was about to take the lifeless brown groper off the tip when I looked up and through the water. About 20 feet away from me, a ten-foot mako shark was sitting there, silently, his dorsal fin splitting the water's surface. He was watching me.

I froze. My mortality came slamming into the back of my head. I ran the numbers: how far am I from the island? How long will it take to get there? What does he want? It's probably the fish he's after.

I pulled the spear up, tore the brown groper off its tip and threw it away from me, so its lifeless, bleeding body drifted down to the bottom of the ocean. The mako did not move. He wasn't interested in that at all.

Right.

My heart started pounding so loudly I could hear it inside my head. I was trying to get my spear sorted so I could use the Powerhead – the Powerhead holds a bullet, in my case a 303 cartridge. When it comes in contact with something, it pushes the body of the Powerhead, and the charge, back onto a firing pin, and that discharges the round. The safety was on and I was stumbling around trying to get the Powerhead out of my shorts, trying to pull the spear up and all of a sudden he flicked out of sight. Gone. Where was he?

I looked around frantically with a quick 360 degree scan across the horizon. Nothing. Slow down, I said to myself and started looking again, more slowly this time. The shark was right behind me. Then – flick – he was in front of me again, moving so fast I could not even see him speed through the water. He covered 50 feet in a flash before coming to another dead stop, facing me again. If he came at me, I wouldn't even have time to move. He shot away again. I spun my head around. Damn, he was right between me and the isthmus.

Into my head tore the words of a friend who had once told me, 'You don't have to worry about sharks until they start circling you.' This one was circling me.

He disappeared again. I knew where to look this time. He had moved 180 degrees back to where he had been originally. I managed to pull the spear back into the gun and fumble through the process of loading the gun, all the time kicking my flippers backwards towards the isthmus. Too slow.

I dropped the sugarbag, my weight belt and the spear gun and started swimming faster than I have ever swum in my life back towards the rocks. As I hit them, Larry grabbed my shoulder and bum and pulled me up.

'You've just been chased out by a shark, haven't you?' he said, laughing.

'Yes,' I panted.

He laughed out loud. 'I have never seen anybody move so fast in all my life. That was incredible.'

We packed up and I sat in the passenger seat shaking all the way home. That had been close. It didn't stop me diving though. When I analysed that dive, I had done everything wrong. The cardinal rules of shark avoidance are: do not dive late in the afternoon because that is when they are feeding; if you are going to, do not dive with a sugarbag leaking a lovely trail of blood into the ocean's veins; and do not dive on your own.

Back on dry land I kept battering away at Margaret every time I had the emotional strength to mount another campaign on the subject of our life together. The day she finally said yes we were both smarting from a bust-up that had taken place after my 21st birthday. I had taken a trip away from Sydney and come back for the October long weekend. I drove round to her place, she eventually turned up, and I asked her yet again: 'Will you marry me?' She said, 'Yes.'

Fantastic, I had a fiancée. My grab at normality had worked. Or at least it looked that way to the outside world. Deep inside me, the demons were still gathering strength.

6

Two years later, at the age of twenty-three, I was an entirely different person. Married, mature, with kids on the way. A successful, respectable businessman. How did I manage that? Strategy, cunning and sleight of hand. It turned out I *had* been learning something at school all those years: how to buck the system.

Everyone assumes you can read – in this day and age why wouldn't they? So you use those assumptions against them. Absolutely critical is keeping close to someone who can do the reading and writing for you. Very close. I married her.

Margaret was my number one asset: practical, capable, unflappable. These days she is an accountant, but even back then if you gave her six columns of figures she would blaze through them like a flame through dry bushland. Supermarket shopping was always fun. She could tell you before you got to the checkout how much you'd be spending and she would be right, every time.

The business she and I bought off my uncle – for $6000, which was a lot back then – was Gymea Produce, handily located in the heart of the southern Sydney suburb of Gymea at the end of a row of shops near a church, so Margaret said it was a godsend. When we walked into the place it was October, the run-up to summer. Our main seller was to be fuel – coke, coal and kerosene – in the winter months. Everybody used to have these fires called cozies, because they kept you cosy, I suppose, and they burnt coke which came from the gasworks, via shops like ours. The gasworks made gas by burning coal.

Wonderful, we thought, handing over a cheque for the shop, becoming tenants in the flat above it and buckling down for a long, tough summer. In those first six months we were so close to going broke we were reduced to eating our own stock – the potatoes, eggs, pumpkins and onions we sold in fits and starts when people couldn't be bothered to go to the grocer's – and I can tell you a lot of ways of cooking those four things. Businesswise, we were really close to the wire. Margaret was our saviour. She studied the books, worked out exactly what we were selling and what wasn't shifting, bought more of the lines that were moving and started increasing the sales margins as much as possible. On a day-to-day level I was the ratbag out the front ordering everyone about; she was the person who did everything else.

Winter came around not a minute too soon and I rang

up the gasworks to order our first batch of coke, the money-spinner that was going to take us through the year, only to hear the words, tinnily apologetic over the phone line: 'There is no more coke. Sorry. Sydney is moving off coke, and onto natural gas.' Natural gas meant no more coal-burning. No more coal-burning meant no more coke. No coke meant no money. We had nothing to sell. Suddenly our $6000 investment looked very ordinary indeed.

I got on the phone and started ringing around; there had to be other gasworks that were not switching over to natural gas. Several hours later, bingo. Maitland. 'But we'll only sell it to you in 13-tonne truckloads, mate,' came the rough-voiced offer down the line.

I had a quick think. 'Why not?' I said. 'Yes, that would be great. Can you deliver?'

The first time they came they left a pile of coke that took up the entire lane at the back of our shop. I had to bag it and shift it all winter long. As the days got colder and shorter, what had looked like a nightmare turned smoothly into a dream. Somehow we were the only produce store around that had managed to get any coke at all. Our turnover went exponential. Instead of selling twenty bags a day I was shifting sixty, so we started getting in two loads at a time and I would pack, stack, pack, stack, onto the back of my truck and deliver it to whoever wanted coke on their doorstep, over and over again. All bloody winter. I would finish every one of those days covered in coke, so after the last run I would shed my clothes as soon as I got into the house and walk stark-naked from the front door into the shower. Coke may be filthy but it washes off easily enough.

Come summer we were expanding the store's range, turning into a produce-cum-pet shop with a lot of garden supplies and plants to boot. The concertina glass doors were pushed back so the whole of the shop opened up, a long narrow space full of fertilisers, chook feed, horse feed, goldfish and white mice, which mainly went to snake owners. We had huge bins full of everything from wheat, oats and corn to phosphate.

When Margaret and I started out, every local town had its own produce store. By the time we had finished, virtually every single one of them in our region was gone. We were it. The closest thing today to what our shop became is one of those old-style stock and station agents in the bush; the place where you go to buy a bale of hay, insecticides, all the bits and pieces you might need for life on the land. Our store was the city version of that, with crossover goods for those still living the country lifestyle; and the smell of the place . . . the smell was just beautiful. A mixture of wheat, grain and blood and bone, a nice earthy aroma. I loved it.

What I had not realised until I started running our shop was that all the time I had been failing to learn to read, I had been picking up other techniques to compensate, and while I would hate anyone to be dyslexic, those skills are very, very useful. There is no Dyslexiaville; we illiterates are forced to live in the world of words. So we learn to think laterally and we get around it. A powerful weapon in our armament is other people's assumptions.

Everybody else always assumes that I am just like them, that if they stuck a piece of paper under my nose and said, 'What do you think of that?' I could tell them. How would they know, just by looking, that I had absolutely no idea?

I was ashamed of my illiteracy – I am ashamed of it still – and I did not want to let anyone else in on the secret. My dyslexia was on a need-to-know basis and as far as I was concerned, nobody needed to know I could not read or write. I certainly was not about to tell anybody. If someone gave me a form I would take it and tell them I would post it back. No way would I reveal the truth to anyone. In one sense, it was hidden very deeply. In another, it was skin-close to the surface.

My paranoia was rampant. When I walked onto a bus in those days, I knew that everybody else on board was talking about me. They were all busy telling each other I was an idiot, a useless, stupid dolt. In life, in business, I always assumed whoever I was dealing with was out to get me, regardless of their real intentions. That they were right and I was wrong. If someone was off with me it was me that was the problem, not them having a bad day or being a ratbag. The diagnosis was dyslexia, but my problem was something much larger than that single word. It was an emotional mountain pressed up against my face, so huge I could not even see it was there.

Margaret helped me hide my condition from the world, and she did it so effectively that I do not remember one single situation where I ended up embarrassed. We never talked about it. It was never that official. We just knew each other so well that she would automatically do things. If there was a form to fill in, she would quietly do it, putting a cross where I needed to sign. It all happened so smoothly, with such a minimum of fuss, that no one ever challenged either of us. Nobody ever thought twice.

When reps came into the store trying to sell us a new product, they would start spinning a line, shoving some brochures under my nose and asking, 'What do you think? Great deal, isn't it? Seen anything as good as these figures? I bet you haven't.'

'Okay,' I'd say. 'I want you to tell me about it, you explain to me what you've got.' They would push the literature at me again and I would say, 'Do you know what, I think Margaret should be in on this. She's my wife and partner, and she's out the back. Hang on a tick, I'll get her. I think you should probably tell us both.'

And Margaret would come out and skim the paperwork while the salesman was talking. We would let him do his spiel, so I'd get the info from him, she'd get it from the paperwork. 'Great,' one or both of us would say, ushering him out the door. 'We'll get back to you.' Margaret would then fill me in on what was written down and we would make our decision.

In banks, post offices, anywhere people would give me forms, I knew that if I even glanced at it they would assume I was speed-reading the thing. So I learnt the skill of looking down as though scanning the document intelligently, looking back up and saying, 'How about I post this back?'

These days I am known largely *because* I have dyslexia. Back when Margaret and I were working together, I was at war with the world. It may have been a cold war, but it was war. We adopted strategies and we defeated the enemy. With her steely eye for detail and my head for strategy, we made our business work. Even so, one of the features of my war was that I could not simply wage the battle and move on. There was always a personal casualty. However inspired and effective my business ideas turned out to be, every form, every piece of literature I came across reminded me of my basic, bottomless failure; of that which I could never do.

Month by month the business grew, prompting my sister Bronwyn and her husband to come in on it. Margaret did the paperwork, Bronwyn kept shop, Wayne looked after the city retail side and I took care of the truck-driving country end. As each local produce shop closed down, our retail dollars increased. We moved into transport, semitrailers, a rough business where the kind of straight-talking that came easily to me is very effective.

Initially I was our main driver – yet another process that other people never think twice about but which is laced with unexploded mines for me. As a kid, if I wanted to go to a beach I would get onto the train that all the people with surfboards under their arms were boarding. If I was off to the city, I would pick the bus with all the suits. If Central Station in the heart of Sydney was my destination, I would head to City Rail and wait on the platform for a sign with a C in it to appear, half the time ending up in Croydon. And that would be one of the good days. More often than not I would only realise as we were zooming down the track that I had just boarded the train to Kogarah by mistake. Cs and Ks always threw me completely.

On a delivery truck run for the business, I was surrounded by signs, the street names clamouring on every corner and intersection. I am completely deaf to those noises, so when I was looking for David Street, the best I could do was find a 'D'. You don't have to be a rocket scientist to be a truck driver, and I learnt early on that it helps to be a real good asker. I stopped taking no for an answer and I overcame my fear of getting it wrong. Looking back on things, I think that the very few people who somehow worked out that I could not read and write thought I could, really; that I was being a bit lazy. Margaret and I would just smile at each other when we realised someone was getting hold of the wrong end of the stick. After all, if it was a business deal, it was usually going to be their funeral.

We both wanted kids, so in November 1972 we got Margaret pregnant. Nine months later, Gayle arrived. I was busy working but the minute Margaret rang from hospital with the sweet, soft words, 'Get your arse up here, I'm going to have it', I catapulted my way there only to be greeted by a blue-clad sister who ushered me into a solarium so lovely and warm that I went to sleep in an old chair as the sun streamed in through the window. Some time later, the nurse woke me up with the words 'Mr Pescud, Mr Pescud. Come and see your daughter', and the moment I set eyes on the little girl, all red and wrinkly, I had the strangest feeling that I had known her forever.

The business kept going, amidst the broken nights, dirty nappies and mewling cries. Margaret kept her eye on all the written stuff while I worked out where we should go next. My skills were the ones that had first started to emerge the day Dad died, and things were working well but emotionally I was wading through sludge – to such an extent that it took almost a year from the date of Gayle's birth before I really became aware of my daughter.

The moment she broke through to me was late one cold, wet Saturday afternoon. Just back from a coke run, I was freezing and soaking wet, with black dust plastered down the length of my back. All I wanted to do was get under a scalding hot shower. The lights in the house were off except for one in Gayle's bedroom, down the end of a long hall, and through her open door I could see the little one-year-old standing in her cot, smiling at me as I walked towards her. That was the first time I realised that Gayle was part of me. I have no idea why, but I became a father that day. Perhaps I needed a gestation period too.

After just over two years of watching Gayle make a playground of the wheat bins, Katie was born. By this time Margaret was busy reading stories to Gayle and I was doing the only thing a decent illiterate father can – making up terrible, tall tales to keep her giggling into her bedsheets.

As the girls grew up I watched them like a hawk for signs of dyslexia. There seems to be a genetic component to the condition which could have been sitting inside the girls' DNA like a time bomb.

Margaret and I started trying to work out where the dyslexia came from. My brother has it to a point, as does one of my cousins. The link seems to be my maternal grandfather who, as far as the family knew, had never read a book. He bought and sold livestock and used to slowly pore his way through the classified section of *The Sydney Morning Herald* looking for stock, but he never attempted to read anything else.

The main thing was, my girls were safe. Katie caught on to reading so quickly it was frightening; she read every book she could lay her hands on, and Gayle was just the same. They had nothing to worry about. Even so, the day Mr Blake walked into my shop, the first thing I thought was, where are they? – a protective reflex as automatic as slamming your hand in front of your child if he or she is in the passenger seat and you have to break suddenly. There he was, chewing his false teeth just the way he'd done when he caned me. But everything seemed telescoped. Mr Blake was so big when I was at school. Here was a tiny guy with no neck, and cheeks that ran into his shoulders. He was fat and soft, and without per-sonality. There seemed to be no character in him, and no suggestion of the violence I knew he was capable of.

Caning someone is a physical thing, but to stand in front of them as the very pinnacle of authority and tell them they are a fat, lazy slob and incompetent and a failure as a person, day in, day out – that is another thing entirely. It was the worst kind of brainwashing at the most impressionable stage of a child's life, and the man standing in my store had done that to me. He was so, so violent.

As I watched him peering into the superphosphate bins, I realised that I was head and shoulders above him. Dickhead Davey Pescud was twenty-six and rock-hard from throwing around 20 tonnes of hay and coke a day. His primary school torturer was neckless, pathetic. I looked at him and thought, how many other people have you done that to?

'Hello, Mr Blake,' I said.

'Er, hello,' the little man replied blankly. He clearly had no idea who I was. He blinked at me in a futile attempt at recognition and smiled vaguely.

I didn't tell him who he was looking at. I did not help him out at all. I let him wander around the shop for a while longer, looking confused. Then he walked out. And I just let him go.

When the girls got to school age, Margaret and I started arguing about where they should go. I wanted to send them to a Montessori school, where I felt they would be listened to and taught to learn, rather than simply taught by rote. Margaret, who had no bad classroom memories at all, insisted we send them to the local primary school so, school bags in hand, off they went.

Gayle and Katie had brought my mother back into the picture. She had no intention of missing out on her grandchildren and our families started spending some real time together for the first time since I had left home. Mum and Rex had a farm, a wonderful playground for the kids and neutral territory for the adults. I started breeding horses, a sideline business that carried on for several years, although our key money-spinner remained the shop and the delivery trucks. The water played its part in that I had a cruising motorboat that we went on for family holidays, but mostly my life was spent on land where, to the untrained eye, things appeared just fine. I had become everything I never thought I could: a good father, a successful businessman and a man in awe of his driven, capable wife.

I couldn't believe it when our marriage started to hit the rocks. I felt like I was being king-hit. However, the girls were seven and five, and I was not about to walk out on them. So we tried to put things back together, attempting to kid ourselves that Camelot was not really lost. Our days were full of anger, recriminations and blame. My nights were plagued with nightmares as all those feelings of insecurity from my youth came tumbling back into my mind.

To this day I am not sure whether the pain of that situation was greater because of my childhood experiences, but it seemed to me that everything I had achieved was a joke. I had failed at this too. So here we go: David Pescud, dyslexic, loser, watches his dad die, keeps things going somehow, meets girl, falls in love, then it all goes wrong. The world had dropped its guts all over me, yet again. It was my fault, I kept telling myself. I should have been better. If I had, none of it would have happened.

Twelve months went by. We sold the core store business and made lots of changes. I became a self-employed subcontractor, a single owner–driver. Materially we were set up beautifully. Money was no problem, we were doing very nicely, thank you. I thought that the children were too young to really understand what was going on, although in hindsight, I do wonder.

At the time I took great pride in not telling anybody. Looking back, that was probably the worst thing I could have done. It did nothing more than trap us inside each other's frailties. In my typically bull-headed way, I wanted to tackle things directly but privately.

So one year's nightmare drifted into two. Before long it was three, and somewhere along the line I just stopped loving her. Or at least, I loved her, but I wasn't in love with her any more. There were lots of things wrong with our relationship. There were an awful lot of things right with us too, in no small part because Margaret was the most matter-of-fact, supportive partner that any man could ask for. If I came home after a day in the trucks and started fibreglassing dinghies, she would be out there with me all night too.

The end crept up on us both, I think. One day I went to a sailing regatta with the wife of a friend of mine, and ended up completely pissed. We wandered back to the boats, I picked her up on my shoulders and threatened to throw her in, and she started giggling. As her peals of laughter echoed from boat to boat, I thought, this is what life should be like – it should be fun, it should be special. And although nothing happened between us that day, it marked the beginning of the end.

There is no point trawling through the divorce proceedings that followed. Suffice to say that I got hammered into a settlement by the family court that resulted in, as far as I was concerned, Margaret ending up with everything that really mattered. She got the kids, the house, the cups and saucers, everything. I got, among other things, the stereo system, the truck – so I could earn enough money to pay her maintenance – and the trailer-sailor. There was no point in trying to fight the court decision; guys all over the country were getting exactly the same deal that was handed down to me.

I slept in that truck at first, having showers at work and getting my clothes cleaned at a laundromat, which all felt incredibly liberating. And there it was. Wealthy one minute, broke the next. That was no real problem – I could build up another small fortune. What I had much more trouble handling was that I no longer had unlimited access to my children. When I separated from Margaret, I never meant to separate myself from them.

The court agreement was like being hit by a hammer emotionally; I suddenly realised I had lost my wife, my house and my kids, and there was no body, no death except the death of our relationship. The upshot was that a perfect stranger could buy my children an ice cream any day of the week but I, their father, could see them only once a fortnight and that was it.

The whole thing was terrible, disgusting, inhumane and uncivilised. Every time I took them home, I died.

I came to hate those second Sunday afternoons more than I can say. Why wouldn't I? After a while I found I was taking my children back to somebody else's house, the house that used to be mine. I'd renovated it, mowed the lawns and done the edges. I'd made the barbecue and had hundreds of parties in it. And there's some other bloke living in there. Because it is not my house any more. Legally. But can anyone really flick a switch and say, 'All these memories I expunge'? They have to.

The woman I had become involved with was wonderful but I was so full of anger, I am surprised she gave me the time of day. I felt so guilty about leaving my children and failing in life that I gave it to her with both spades. Within two months of us getting together we did the horribly obvious thing and set up our own home in Mascot. I then proceeded to make her life hell, lying to her every way you can lie. I don't think I ever treated anyone so badly as that; I hope to God I never do again.

She had children too, and we would have all our kids on the same weekend. It made sense. They would get to know each other and we could spend those weekends at Joyce and Rex's farm. We would all drive back to Sydney on Sunday afternoon. I'd drop my kids off at their mother's, she would drive off separately to say goodbye to her children and drop them off at their father's. By the time she got back to the place we shared, I would have downed half a bottle of Scotch to ease the pain. She would walk in and pour herself a large glass of port, and that was that. Every second Sunday.

We split up after about six months: she moved out

and I moved away, to the nearby suburb of Oatley, and I had a think. I had lost more than the house and kids in the marriage breakdown. Margaret had been my number one asset for thirteen-odd years, my armour against the world, and without her I was stripped naked. I was on my own. Social situations that previously would never have been a problem turned into time bombs. I would go to people's houses and, say, be invited to play Scrabble. I've got a good vocabulary, so it made sense to them but, boy, the excuses I would have to make to get out of such situations before I got into them. I would try to put somebody else on the spot: 'Oh no, Roger's better than me, he should do it,' or 'Sorry, mate, I'll only be here a few minutes, I've really got to run.' Once I got spectacles I realised I could have spent my whole life saying, 'Oh, I'd love to but I haven't got my glasses with me.' Damn, I wish I had known about that earlier.

One particularly cringeworthy event happened at a dinner party full of people I didn't know – elite academics, actors and the head of the Australian Broadcasting Corporation. Somebody started a game around the table in which the first person had to write a line of verse on a piece of white card, then hand it over to the person beside them, who read it out loud, wrote a line to complement it, then handed it on again. The game started on the other side of the table and was travelling relentlessly towards me. I was thinking, I'll go to the loo, I'll spill the soup all over my belly, I'll bloody fake a fit, something, anything. The girl I was with knew my problem but she wasn't Margaret, who would have headed something off like this at the pass, and I knew I was basically on my own.

I was in a cold sweat, watching this card get closer, and at the same time trying to work out what I was going to say without having a clue as to how I was going to write it – or how I was going to tell everyone I couldn't write it. So my brain's in gear working out how to create this line, knowing I can't, waiting to be emotionally harpooned at the same time. It was a nightmare; the card was getting closer and closer, like some horrible slow-motion car crash scene in a movie. A glimmer of hope appeared as I listened to the direction of the verses. I thought, I can do this.

The card finally hit the woman in an evening dress sitting next to me, an actress from *Number 96*. She wrote something down that she said flicked the meaning off in a different direction and handed it to me. I couldn't read a word she'd written. What was I going to do? I took the only route left open to me. I looked at it quickly, leant over to the actress and quietly said: 'Can you do a favour for me? I can't read and write, so would you read out what you've written, then write down what I say?'

She looked stunned but complied, without a word. Everyone at the table must have picked up on what was going on but nothing was said and the card continued on its merry way around what was left of the table until the game collapsed under its own weight.

I broke out in a sweat. I'd dealt with it but all I wanted to do was dive into a hole in the ground. My fellow guests were very polite, too polite to even mention it. After all, they had done the wrong thing by putting me on the spot. That didn't make it any easier for me, though, and I was very, very glad to pick up my coat and get out of there.

Some dyslexics go to restaurants and order by numbers, because it's the only way they can. I never have. Left alone, I can quietly stumble through a menu. I might see the word 'lamb' and go for that; then 'fruit' – great, I'll have that. As soon as anyone got involved in my life, though, I would tell them because ultimately I would need them to help. I did the best I could. It was difficult. I took forms back to Mum, who was devastated by the break-up, and I made sure I always had a girlfriend lurking around somewhere to help me out.

I had enough experience to know when a deal was sweet and worth spinning, and one of the positive things that came out of the break-up was that it left me foot-loose. As good as Margaret was in business, working with her slowed me down. Alone I could make decisions fast. I could do what made sense without having to discuss it. So that is what I did.

I began truck subcontracting seriously as an owner–driver. I subcontracted with Ansett at a time when contracts weren't worth a brass razoo, but the pay was excellent. I learnt to fill in the all-important log books by copying words from my map book – 'Destination . . . Brisbane'. I could identify the words coming up at me on a motorway at 100 clicks by seeing the B, and the I, and maybe there's an S, so I would guess this was the turnoff and get into the left-hand lane. After a while I even started spelling the words correctly. Weekends and early mornings I spent doing other jobs, like delivering produce to market. Life was sweet, financially.

Things started looking up on the emotional front as well. I met the proverbial older woman: Margaret Lapthorne was her real name, Maggie Stuart was her stage name. She was a singer. She rented a flat downstairs in a house that I was living in upstairs, in Oatley. She was the girl that changed it all.

Now, Maggie was somewhat bewildered as to why she was not more 'successful in life', meaning with money, basically. When it comes to organising your affairs, making cash and making it work for you – all those things I found so easy – she was utterly useless. In terms of living skills and the important things of life, however, she is probably the smartest person I have ever been involved with. I remember asking her what her definition of intelligence was. She replied: 'Broadmindedness.' At the time I said something smart like 'What?', but the more I think about her answer, the more I suspect she was probably right.

She was the first person to try to convince me that I was not a failure and I felt she really listened to me. I got the impression that she respected me and I found myself responding with respect. We had a series of conversations in which I started pouring my heart out to her, telling her about my father and how I felt my mother had abandoned me. I had always believed I was ugly, that I only managed to lure women anywhere near me by

force of personality, and that they weren't really interested in me at all. She asked me if I'd ever been knocked
back by a girl, and the answer was no.

'So,' she said, 'if you're so unattractive, why haven't
they knocked you back?'

I came up with some lame excuse, because I had a nice
car or something, but she wasn't having any of it. Then
one day I decided to write something for her. When I say
'write' I mean dictate onto tape. A poem. I swallowed
my pride and gave it to her

'This is beautiful,' she said. 'Really, really beautiful.
You are very good with words. You speak well, you com-
municate well, you get your emotions and feelings across
to people well.'

'Get out of here,' I told her, but I let her type the poem
up anyway. That poem is lost now, which is a real shame.
I wish I'd kept a copy of it.

Then Maggie started quizzing me about work, saying
that I must have a very sound head for business.

'No, I was just lucky,' I said. 'I had a good wife and
business partner.'

'Yeah . . .' came the reply. 'But you started it, you ran it.
You two were a partnership but the enterprise might not
have happened if it hadn't been for you.'

I had never considered it that way. I'd always thought
that I'd just been in the right place at the right time, that
any success was down to somebody else. Even so, there
has always been this crazy undercurrent in me that has
said, and goes on saying, you can do anything.

At twenty-two I didn't think I was a failure, I knew it.

I was doing things, starting things, but if anyone said 'Well done', I would say 'It's down to my wife', or 'Luck', or something. By thirty-four, everything had broken down in my life and I was ready, I suppose, to reassess things. So when Maggie told me I should see a therapist, I listened to her.

At 5 pm one afternoon, I made my way to a single-storey, red-brick Federation house in Hurstville. I remember thinking, mmm, it's on the eastern side of the road, it would have a very sunny back yard, I'd like that, before starting the long, slow march up the very short path to the front door. Deep-set leadlights in the windows stopped me peering inside, so I took a big breath, knocked on the door and waited.

A chic little old lady with short grey hair – the last thing I had been expecting – peered at me from behind the solid front door. 'You must be David,' she said. 'I'm Val. How are you?' We shook hands.

'Come in.'

7

I HAVE TWO HISTORIES, one marked by births, marriage and deaths.

The other is marked by boats.

It began when my father moved us to the water's edge and stopped abruptly when Margaret turned up on the scene and decided sailboat racing – something I was into pretty heavily back then – was not for her. I gave it up, too, for about a decade. That was a bad decision. I loved diving but after we got married my back started playing up and I was forced to give it away.

By the time my relationship with Margaret had hit its final, turbulent phase and I went back to work as a sub-contractor, I had all but forgotten what it was about. Then Alan Cooper, who was still my best friend, bought a sailboat. Alan had one marriage behind him, another on the way out and was busy working his way towards his third. He had bought a sailboat, turned up in Sydney with his girlfriend – he lived in Canberra at the time – and said, 'Let's go sailing.'

It had been around ten years since I had sailed on a boat but I really had not missed it. I turned up at Gunnamatta Wharf as agreed, hopped on the boat and motored down the bay past the fisheries. Alan and I lifted the sail up, and suddenly the boat caught the wind, leant over and started to move. It was one of those defining moments; everything clicked. I knew that I was exactly where I belonged. I was a sailor. I would always be a sailor. I can still feel the rush now, and every time I go sailing, it's the same. I get a tingle. I had forgotten that however bad I was feeling, I could always still get out onto the water.

That was a Saturday. On Monday it was pouring down with rain and I was counting the days until I could sail again. Alan and I were in and out of boats nonstop after that. I had a boat shed and people would ask if they could keep their craft in there when they weren't using them. Sure, I would say. Then as soon as their backs were turned, we'd be out. Then I upped the ante and started actually building the buggers.

The first boat I built was *Alternative*, a Pacific 747 that came in moulds ready to be put together. It was 24 feet long and a dog: fine for caravanning the family around but needing a cyclone behind it to get anywhere. *Alternative 2* was another trailer-sailor, a Tympany 770 and a great boat. It worked for the family and sailed nicely, so we kept that for quite a few years. Then came the divorce. I got rid of *Alternative 2* and started building *Pax*. I suppose the boat was a symbol of what I was searching for. There was no peace then, except when I was working on the boat.

I had failed with my wife, lost my kids, fallen in love again and buggered up that second relationship. I had told lies, treated women badly and killed off my chance at happiness. My hurt told me there would never be another love like the ones I had already experienced: probably a little melodramatic, but I was hurling blame and abuse at myself so hard there was no calm in my life. No stillness.

Until I went to the boat and started working on it once more.

Every time I got out there, with my blues box blaring, I would start chopping up wood and telling lies to all the other guys making boats about how we were going to sail across the world. I meant it, though. I was building the boat I would disappear on. It would take me across the seven seas for the rest of my life.

The boat-building skills I was honing weren't new to me. What was going on in therapy was. As Val asked me question after question and nudged me into picking my life apart, I realised that if the skills I relied upon to keep me afloat emotionally were chisels, half the time I was picking them up by the wrong end and cutting myself.

At first I saw Val once a week. I kept it quiet from my fellow boat-builders; in fact I didn't tell anyone except my sister Bronwyn, and I certainly didn't let on what was happening in those sessions. I never told her what Val was like – she was probably in her sixties and well-dressed in a smart, David Jones way. A little bit twee with a blouse, skirt and scarf, but she was well turned out. Professional, with something of a swing to her. She reminded me a bit of my mother.

In that first session she showed me into a neat, well-lit room – one I would get to know so well – leading off the hallway and gestured to one of two big armchairs opposite a desk where pieces of paper were tidily stacked up. It was in her home but it didn't look like anybody's room. It was academically clinical.

'What are you here for, David?' she said, sitting down. Light streamed through the window behind me, seeming to focus her enquiry into a pencil-beam spotlight.

'I've been referred,' I said, hedging.

'Yes, that's fine, David.' She looked at me with her sharp, intelligent face. I gazed at my palms, callused from working on the boat. My eyes darted towards the arm-chairs, the carpet – anything but her.

'Now, David, why do you want to see me?'

Sod it, I thought, and blurted it out: 'I want to know what is real. I don't understand who I am.' It was as simple as that.

On one level our sessions were just talking, and Val wanted to know everything. She had this knack of asking one or two questions, then sitting back for half an hour while the floodgates opened. For weeks I thought, this is bullshit, it's not going anywhere. Then – bang – I was stumbling over myself and under-standing what it was all about. I felt like a six-year-old who keeps falling over and doesn't realise until he stands up that he has taken the skin off both knees so badly he is bleeding all over the pavement.

Val told me that of the many things I had become, I was also the sum total of what I had been put through. She used an image of a big vase. 'Think about all the things that were put into that vase,' she would say, and I'd think, Christ. No wonder I was fucked up. I was drowning in there.

A more useful image came later, when I realised that emotionally I was completely in the dark, and that I had been stumbling about in the pitch-black for so long, I had bleeding shins and broken toes. Val gave me a torch. She showed me how to light up the room I had locked myself into. Deep inside, against one of the back walls of that imaginary room, there was a mirror. I began dancing around that mirror, looking at the back, the top, the sides, then finally sneaking in front for a quick glance at myself.

When we got to my childhood and my developing illiteracy, I was overwhelmed by how much I felt I had been let down by the school, even by my parents. I found myself blaming my mother, Joyce. Memories started tumbling over themselves, of copping it at school, then copping it at home. I realised that in some ways I am very dumb. I never wagged school, for example; I turned up every single day. Why did I bother? But that is what I did, and in the process I ended up taking what school was doling out on the chin much more than I otherwise might have.

I found myself recalling little episodes, conversations between my mother and myself when I was tiny, or at school. It must have been terribly difficult for my parents because they were bright – they both went to selective schools – and there was I, their oldest child, apparently unable to learn. Erudite things were discussed in our household. My parents initiated conversations about the arts, politics, philosophy, so to have this son who could discuss things but could not grapple with the written word must have been a real trial. Well, I was never like other kids; I never could be. I was never good enough. My parents told me school was a good thing, my school told me I was a dickhead. QED.

One day I had a toothache and was crying a lot, and Mum told me: 'You have a really low pain threshold.' Years later, an accident left a semitrailer lying square on my back. I was doing my best to keep conscious through the searing pain and I thought, I don't think my pain threshold is that low at all. As the truck bore down on me, I started laughing, even while every system in my body was fighting to keep going.

When Val and I started peeling back the years and finding what lay at the root of my rock-bottom self-esteem and violent behaviour, I remember her saying, 'Sit in front of this chair and pretend this chair is your mother. Now, tell her what you are feeling.'

My reaction was, I'm not going to talk to a fucking chair, but Val coaxed me into it and maybe it worked because one Australia Day long weekend when I had the kids at Mum and Rex's farm, a really strange shift took place. I really loved those weekends and was very jealous of my time with the girls, but I was off on a boat, an important regatta in Sydney Harbour, and Mum had been looking after them. As I made my way into the farm and walked inside to find everybody, my stepfather spotted me and said, 'You're in trouble.'

'How can I be?' I said.

'You'd better get upstairs and see your mother.'

I walked into the kitchen where she was waiting, and got both barrels. She blasted me. What had happened was that she had had all her grandchildren at the farm that weekend, and the kids had run amuck. Kate, my youngest, was eight and the kind of character who could quite happily start World War III before breakfast. Gayle was a very responsible individual, it was as though she was put here to say 'How can I make your life better?' Kate was going through a phase where she might as well have been put here to say 'How can I wreck it?'

So I walked in and my mother threw everything at me. She just let rip. She said, 'I wish your children were more like your sister's children,' and my knees went weak.

I thought, I've heard this before.

Then a rare thing happened. For the first time in my life, I went into this third-person mode. Mum was beside the sink, I was in front of the cupboard, and while she was reading the riot act to me, a second me was standing a few feet away, watching her furious face, hearing her angry words and listening to Val at the same time. Any other time I would have fired back at her with both barrels plus interest, but I found myself thinking, oh shit, it's true. All the stuff about the comparisons, it really is all true.

That was the day I started to excuse myself. Up until then all the stuff Val and I had talked about was nebulous, somehow abstract, as though it did not really have anything to do with me. Suddenly I couldn't deny anything any more. Mum used to compare me unfavourably to other people sometimes. I had talked about it at length with Val and she told me it was probably still happening. It was, but to my own kids. As the therapy finally started making sense of the tensions between us, the effect was overwhelming. I drove the girls back to their mother's house, and for once I could not wait to get there. Usually I loathed Sunday afternoons with a vengeance, but on that day I needed to be on my own and try to calm the storm that had exploded in my head.

I reacted with embarrassment, for her. I didn't say much – it was too big, somehow – I just swept up the kids and left. But it changed the way I behaved towards her forever. That day, she turned into a human being in my eyes, rather than an infallible parent. It was the beginning of my being able to treat her as an equal. We had a chat about it some months later and then went through several fairly turbulent years of readjustment. I consider her one of the most fantastic people on the planet and our relationship now is much, much stronger.

As the months went by and Val's weekly sessions continued, Mags and I gradually went our separate ways, breaking up after about a year together. We were hopelessly incompatible, really. She doesn't move until twelve o'clock, while I am an early morning person. We had a purpose to being together and I will always be eternally grateful to her for making me think that I wasn't a total loser. She made me realise there was more to me than that.

Meanwhile, the boat *Pax* grew from a skeleton into the half-fleshed version of what she would eventually become. I, on the other hand, was turning into a deconstructed version of the man I had been when I first walked into her house. Our sessions were paring me back to my core, until my once full-bodied personality felt like little more than a bleached pile of bones.

I realised that the dyslexia was like a constant strain, like white noise. Part of the reason I started talking to Val was my confusion. What was I really capable of? I mean, I can't read a book but I can find a way of getting it read to me. If someone said, 'Go to the moon,' I reckon I could find a way up there. I had no trouble making decisions about money, snapping up a waterfront unit in Sylvania for a mere $82,000 without a second thought. Yet I appeared handicapped to the rest of the world. After all, if you want to know about sailing, what's the first thing you do? Find a book? Check it out on the Internet? Okay, now imagine you want to know about sailing but you can't read. What do you do? You talk to people. But who? Say you manage to get in touch with a sailing club and talk to someone, how do you know the fellow you are talking to is any good? You don't, but you go with it anyway.

Next thing you know you are on a boat, asking someone, 'What's a halyard?' They tell you it is the rope, or wire, that is used to lower and hoist the sails. Then you say, 'So what's a lanyard?' 'A short line attached to one object that secures it to another,' comes the reply. Later that evening you try to remember. What *is* a halyard? If you can't answer the question now, there is no way of finding out. You are stuck. Reading a book means being able to look it up, any time of day or night. If you can't, when someone tells you something, you have got to remember it. Lock it up, baby, because you can't be sure you are going to get another chance to ask. If you are very fortunate someone might assist you, but you can not rely on it.

You become very nervous of asking people for the thousandth time. You try to remember everything and you can not, so you throw information out of the back of your head to enable you to keep more in the front. Then you start prioritising. If that is not hard enough, you are continually working through this emotional fog of failure while you are doing it all. For me that fog began to lift when I started having therapy.

My wife Margaret worked my life in such a way that no one needed to know, and that was all right with me because I was ashamed of it. I am ashamed still. I did not want anyone else to know my disgusting secret, and while Margaret was around they did not have to. When she left, the background noise that was dyslexia became deafening, and I had to learn to deal with it all over again.

Val and I continued on this journey that had a lot to do with self-esteem, in the end. I tend to think of it in terms of a camera, the lens of which has 20,000 filters in front of it. What Val started doing was peeling off those filters, or letting me peel them off, one by one, until eventually I realised that the camera was focused on me, and while I never made the prettiest of pictures, I wasn't going to crack the lens either.

We talked about the losing of Camelot – my break-up with Margaret – and I started to realise that the two of us had worked together well but we had always had very different styles. Even the first dinner party we gave showed it. Everything was absolutely perfect, just the right number of knives, the table setting looking so pristine that had I been a guest I would have been scared to move in case I wrecked it. The table was a work of art.

That was Margaret's way of doing things. I am different. A dinner party at my house means there might be a tablecloth, there might not. What there will be is a massive bowl of spaghetti, a truckload of the best salad in the world, so much fresh bread you won't know what to do with it, three or four really nice sauces and a huge plate of great antipasto. You can kick your shoes off, mess your hair up and say 'G'day' to everybody in the room. For me life is about people and being friends and taking the time to find out about each other. Such realisations were very emotionally turbulent for me. At times it felt like creating a wound in my body, my soul, as though I was tearing my chest open. Then I let someone stick their head in and look around. It really hurt.

So after two years of sessions with Val, *Pax* was built and I could not take the pain of therapy any more. I came to this realisation as I was driving around delivering things in the truck. I stopped for lunch at the back of Fairfield. I had been gradually thinking that I had had enough and that I was on the right track, that I could help myself from now on, but none of that was at the forefront of my mind. My feet were up on the steering wheel and as I munched my sandwich I turned the radio on and started listening to the cricket. Australia seemed to be doing okay in a slow, frustrating kind of way.

Across in a large field was a solitary cow, chewing on its own lunchtime version of a sandwich, and apropos of absolutely nothing, I suddenly felt as though I had been hit on the back of the head with a cricket bat. A physical tremor went through my body and I realised enough was enough. The answers I was looking for with Val were inside me. Simple as that. If I asked myself for help, I would get it. I could help myself. Trite but true. The third person that had invisibly appeared in the kitchen with Mum that day had grown, and there were several Davids now, including one that watched things constantly. He did not always have the answer, but he could offer some perspective.

My first question to Val had been 'What is real?' My answer was, 'It all is.' People will tell you I am a hard man. I have heard that a lot in my life, so I guess it must be true. Well, I am much harder on myself than I am on anyone else, and that understanding certainly helped me get closer to the people who counted – my family. The David who had gone into therapy wanting to know what was real came out of it more confident, though by no means as confident as he thought he was at the time. He was more at ease with himself, and understood better that whatever happened, he was alright. He wanted to know more about himself and had taken several steps in a journey that would carry on for the rest of his life.

The idea that I was stupid because I could not read was starting to recede, but it was still there. My kneejerk reactions were changing though. One time I was driving a semitrailer across some traffic lights and the guy in front stopped, leaving me straddled across the grid-locked intersection. There was a taxi beeping on his horn but by that time there was absolutely nothing we could do. I had stuffed up. It happens.

I climbed out of the truck absolutely furious with the taxi driver and crossed the road to confront him. He stayed put in his car, his big shiny head cowering beneath the roof. He was terrified I was going to bang him. I did not. I put a hand on each of his ears and kissed him on the forehead, turned around and marched back to my truck. Two years earlier I would have gone over to the taxi driver, dragged him out of his car and thrown him into Sydney Harbour. Then I would probably have let his handbrake off.

People really can change.

So, as the finishing touches to *Pax* went on, I finally said goodbye to Val's red-brick terrace. The boat was fitted out and ready to drop into the water. She was a 34-foot, three-quarter tonner. Originally designed as a racing yacht, I was going to cruise in her, so I had made a lot of modifications. I thought that was going to be my boat, the one that would take me through the rest of my life, so I put her in the water and started sailing her.

Then I met Susan, wife number two. We found each other in the oddest place. Out clubbing – something I never normally do.

It was a Saturday night at the Intersection, a very famous nightspot where I come from. I had been talked into the whole thing by a couple of mates who ignored my cries of 'I'm not going there, it's full of desperate people' and dragged me in anyway. It got to midnight and I was ready to go. Paul had started chatting up this woman and I said, 'I'm out of here, see ya.' I flashed a quick final look towards the bar and saw the back of a remarkable head of hair falling onto some fine shoulders – very well-groomed, beautifully presented. Blonde, of course.

Wanting to know what was on the other side of that hair, I bought a drink and took a circuitous route back, doing the long-range checkout by peeking behind other people in the crowd; seeing without being seen, I thought.

'What *are* you up to?' said Paul when I finally got back, snorting into what was left of his beer. I pointed Susan out.

'Mmm,' he said. 'I see what you mean.'

The long and short of it is that Susan picked me up in the end. She had been out with her housemates for a meal that night and they'd been looking for somewhere to have drinks afterwards. She started chatting to me about the music being played, then we had a bit of a dance and before I could think, God, she's attractive,

I was back at my bachelor pad entertaining what felt like a cast of thousands – she had brought some mates with her for protection – when all I wanted to do was put my arm around her.

The next day she disappeared off to the snow for a week's skiing – the worst week I'd had for ages – and before I knew it we were an item. At that point I was running my own business with half a dozen trucks, which meant I was fairly free to come and go as I pleased, so we scooted off to art galleries, had slow sensuous dinners and stayed up so long we'd end up watching the sun rise.

Within six weeks we were serious and I asked her to marry me. I was very quick about it, all hot and bothered. She said 'Yes' and that was that. I was really, really happy. In the four years since my wife and I had split I had had a few girlfriends but none had really stuck. Then along came this woman who was not only beautiful but intelligent – a librarian, of all things. Too many of the women I'd been meeting had been to school, gone to work for a couple of years as secretaries or teachers, got married, had kids and switched their brains off. All they would do was talk about their kids, or bitch about their ex, and while that can be fun, it stopped me getting to know them.

Susan, on the other hand, was educated and very well-read. She had an opinion on everything but she listened too, and really asked questions. Within half an hour of meeting her I told her I was dyslexic. Before the counselling I might not have done that, not because the sessions with Val had made me feel it was okay to say it – rather, they made me feel it was un-okay not to. As soon as I met Susan I felt she was going to be important so I blurted it out, because if she couldn't deal with it, I needed to know.

Everything started happening very fast. We planned to get married, start cruising and have a family. *Pax* was not big enough for that so I sold it for $95,000 and started knuckling down on the skeleton of the new boat, a 54-footer that took me two and a half years to build. We called it the *Carpe Diem*: Seize the Day.

Counselling was over but its effects persisted, like a rock thrown into the water. It sent out ripples that went on and on; they bounced off the shoreline and came back in different ways, at different frequencies. Much more subtly. When I met Susan I had convinced myself that I was better equipped to deal with a new relationship. I did all the right things. I decided she was my girl, I told her my secrets. She was nine years younger than me, and she'd always been free to do exactly what she wanted. I came along and said, 'I've been married, I'll show you how to do it.' Very stupid of me. Her response was, 'No, no, no. This is how you do it.'

She moved in with me three months after we met and we couldn't keep our hands off each other. It was that type of relationship, passion one minute, throwing things the next. The arguments were enormous, then the next minute we'd be in bed going as hard as we could.

Then we got dropped into a set of circumstances that changed everything. In September or thereabouts,

Susan's mother Jean – who had been through breast cancer three or four years beforehand – was diagnosed with secondary cancer. The prognosis was not good. Tony, Jean's husband, was faced with a tragedy of enormous proportions. His mate was going to die. Susan's response was to rush forward the wedding so that Jean could be there. It was pretty obvious she was going to die before the year was out, so we didn't worry too much about the fact that we were arguing like cats and dogs because when we weren't, we were cuddling all the time. Suddenly it was all about Jean and trying to support Susan's family as much as we could.

I don't think I did as good a job as I could have. I was making demands on Susan, she was leaning on me and at the same time becoming more and more torn between me and her family. Had I been a bit more circumspect, I would have said, 'No, we're not going to get married. Let's spend time with your mother and see what we've got; see what's real.' But Susan was desperate to have her mum at the wedding so we set the day for early December. Her mother took the wind out of everybody's sails by passing away in November. By then it was too late to cancel the wedding so we went ahead anyway.

It was a lovely day in the end, very emotional as you can imagine. Susan walked down the aisle looking like the most lovely thing on the planet, and my knees went gooey. Later that evening she appeared in a beautiful black nightie. We were used to seeing each other's bodies, but that night I was going to bed with my wife. Things were perfect. I never wanted anything to change.

Needless to say, the relationship started going down-hill pretty quickly. I sold my place in Sylvania and focused my energies on finishing the boat that was going to take us cruising around the world. But before too long, Susan had walked out a couple of times, then her grandma came out here from England and stayed with us. Hilda was a lovely little 85-year-old lady, but she wasn't used to creepy-crawlies. She couldn't even stand black beetles when she was in England.

I had just bought a place at Grays Point – water glimpses, brick cottage, very peaceful – and I'd said, 'Let's zap the place with insecticide before we move in.' Susan didn't want to. I had this stuff down on the farm which was a little bit naughty but very effective. I told her, 'I'll bring down some gear, we'll spray the place inside and outside, leave it to settle and move in when we're ready.'

'No way,' she said. 'That is not going to happen.' So it didn't and we had cockroaches – so many that Susan would later joke about having to turn the television up so we could not hear them dancing around in the drawers.

Late one night a huge ruckus erupted from Hilda's room. I was in bed, stark naked and tangled up in my wife's sleepy legs, and suddenly this 85-year-old lady was screaming her head off. I tore myself awake, pulled some pants on and raced into her room.

Hilda was up and staggering towards the door with her little old lady's nightgown on and an expression of sheer terror on her face. There was one cockroach on her face and another on her shoulder, and poor old Hilda was having a coronary. I thought it was the funniest thing I had ever seen in my life. I just hooted with laughter.

By now Susan had come around the corner. She did the sensible thing and went for the cockroaches, brushing them firmly off her grandmother. Hilda was very upset. She moved out the following week. From there our relationship headed into the deep south very quickly. I think we were in marriage guidance counselling within six months of our wedding day. I was all fired up about counselling, I thought it could help you fix anything. Sadly not.

We tried a few counsellors and they always started out by saying the same thing, 'What is wrong with your marriage?', which always struck me as the wrong question. Why not ask a warring couple, 'What's right with your marriage?' Why chuck more cold water on things?

One of them asked Susan why she had married me. Good question.

'Because he will make a good father,' she replied.

There are points in your life where you go, bong – wrong answer. As a relationship slides away from you, you kid yourself it will get better. Then one simple statement like that and the mist clears. I thought, that is not why I married you, and that is not why I thought you married me. Yeah, I will be a good father but I married you because I want to be with you. That is why I am here.

The anguish crept up on me and tied itself into a big knot around the fact that we loved each other but the relationship was just not working. I was jealous and made big demands on her, which threatened her, I think. She withdrew, I got more worried, made more demands and the whole relationship spiralled further and faster out of control.

Maybe there was too much going on. In the middle of all this I got a phone call from my daughters one day asking if they could come and live with me. Instead of doing the right thing – sitting everybody involved down in a family circle with Margaret, her husband John, Susan and all the kids to talk out a proper arrangement – I stupidly just said 'Yes'.

Gayle was fifteen and careering towards her HSC. Kate was two years younger. Yes, I realised it was going to be a handful, but I hadn't considered just how big a change it would mean. I was in the habit of getting out of bed in the morning starkers, putting the coffee on, and walking past Susan, who would also be starkers, into the shower. Suddenly our lives were not our own. We were in pyjamas and the kids were in the shower. It was something I wanted but I did have trouble adjusting.

When Gayle hit sixteen she was dux of her year in languages and went to Japan for six weeks on an exchange program, leaving Kate in our house on her own. It can't have been easy for her with us having regular shouting matches, but it was still Susan who was bearing the brunt emotionally. Her mother had died not all that long ago and she hadn't really even started dealing with things. After little more than two tumultuous years, our relationship was buried with her and Susan finally moved out of our Grays Point home, never to return. The girls were sorry about it but not too surprised.

My family remain close to Susan, who came to Gayle's wedding and still goes to Mum's for dinner. She has shared baby clothes with Katie. After we broke up, she bought a unit up near Sutherland where she worked, and we were still seeing each other, inasmuch as she would come to the farm every now and again. There are lots of bunk beds up there but I remember one night when Susan took one of the double beds and I found myself really wanting to get into bed with her. I didn't though.

Back at Grays Point, our lives continued. At eighteen, Gayle went back to Japan for a year on a Rotary exchange program, coming back to do a BA, specialising in Japanese, at Sydney University. She was being enriched beyond imagination by her education, which was wonderful to watch, but it did remind me that just one generation before all this, my own schooling had very nearly destroyed me.

She stayed with me until she moved out to live with Jason, who she later married. Katie, who did not enjoy school and got an exemption to leave before the end of Year 10, came and went, but my place remained her base until she moved out into share accommodation in her early twenties.

Susan and I didn't get divorced until she met the man she wanted to spend the rest of her life with. Our relationship had been over for several years by then. It was sad when we finally separated legally. I was about forty-five and pretty glad to be out of it in a way, because it had been painful.

I did not really need to work any more, thanks to the sale of my business. So I threw myself back into finishing off the *Carpe Diem*, little realising that my life was about to change forever.

8

I HAD NO IDEA I WAS on a mission until December 1993. The scene was Sydney's beachside suburb of Coogee: I was drinking lukewarm coffee with sawdust in it and helping a mate called John build a boat in his sun-drenched back yard. The radio was switched on to the ABC, as it usually is when I'm working, so news, views and current affairs wafted about in the mid-afternoon breeze as we slowly put John's catamaran together. Presenter John Doyle was busy putting his guests through their paces. At the back of my mind I realised one of those interviewees was talking about sailing. He wanted to participate in the Sydney to Hobart yacht race, he said. Not only was it one of the world's major sporting events, watched by millions of people every year, the course stood as one of the toughest and potentially most perilous ocean races on the planet, and he was really keen to compete.

Well, there's nothing unusual about that. Any sailor worth their salt would sell their grandmother twice over for a chance to crew on one of the boats lined up for that particular excursion. This guy was different, though. He was paraplegic, and loved the idea of a disabled crew doing the race. What skipper in his right mind would take him? I put down my tools and had a listen. The would-be sailor wasn't just anyone, he was Phil Vardy, the scientist who had blown the whistle on Australia's notorious thalidomide doctor, William McBride.

Vardy was a boy from Murwillumbah in northern New South Wales who, at twenty-four years old, had had a motorbike crash that broke his back and lodged him in a wheelchair. Never one to be stopped in his tracks, he finished his biology degree and started looking for work. He managed to secure a job with Sydney practitioner Dr William McBride, who was well known and lauded for his work on thalidomide, the drug taken by pregnant women in the fifties and sixties which resulted in thousands of deformed foetuses and children. McBride's research had uncovered the malforming effects of thalidomide, leading to the drug being banned and McBride receiving international acclaim.

One of McBride's new interests was Debendox, an anti-nausea drug used by pregnant women. He asked Vardy to do some experiments on pregnant rabbits but when Vardy realised how his employer had written up the research in a scientific journal – changing the drug dosages and adding fictitious rabbits to back up his assertion that the drug might be damaging foetuses – he confronted him and promptly lost his job. After much agonising, Vardy went public several years later, ending McBride's career in a storm of revelations that resulted in the great doctor's fall from grace. In 1993, McBride was barred from practising. (He would be reinstated years later when the New South Wales Medical Tribunal found it was in the public interest.)

As new rules swept through the Australian research community making it harder to get away with scientific fraud, Vardy was lauded as a hero. But the McBride affair took its toll. Vardy's career slowed and his marriage disintegrated. Once the dust settled, he started rebuilding his life.

Vardy got to know Peter Aspinal, a sight-impaired sailor, and before long the two joined forces with another able-bodied friend and started sailing on Sydney Harbour. Vardy had learnt the basics of sailing before his accident, during a visit to the Davis Base in Antarctica in 1971, where he experimented with ice yachting, and later at university.

As he got to grips with the ropes on Sydney Harbour, he started thinking about the Sydney to Hobart yacht race. The ABC radio appearance was a call to arms, a challenge, and as I listened to his quiet determination and sipped what was left of my sawdust-filled coffee, I thought, why not?

I phoned Phil Vardy and told him if he really wanted a boat, I had one. The *Carpe Diem* was finally finished – a beautiful 54-foot cruising ship that was going to take me around the world. Even so, I was starting to think that a slight detour from my plan to disappear over the horizon might not hurt. Regular racing with normal crews had become boring, and I did need a new challenge.

Before we knew it, Vardy, I and a dozen or so of the other people who had got in touch with him after his radio interview were sitting at my house in Grays Point, introducing ourselves and working out what to do next. The goal was clear: to take a disabled crew into the 1994 Sydney to Hobart yacht race. No one in the world had ever attempted that, to our knowledge. They had certainly never achieved it. That was it, then. That was exactly what we would do.

Having the boat was the lynchpin – without the *Carpe Diem*, we couldn't do anything. But a boat that is ready to go cruising and one set up for ocean racing are two entirely different animals. Turning one into the other was going to take some serious money, and that meant sponsorship.

We did some sums and worked out that $50,000 would get us to Hobart. That covered insurance and race entries but we targeted the biggest chunk by far – around $25,000 – at fitting out the boat with safety equipment, life-rafts, first aid kits, flotation devices and harnesses, as well as racing sails. We needed what is known in sailors' parlance as a wardrobe of ten or fifteen racing sails, every one tailor-made for the *Carpe Diem*, the name of which was becoming more appropriate by the day.

Talking of names, we needed one for the new-found organisation. The title 'Sailors with disAbilities' came up after Phil Vardy workshopped ideas around with someone else. It was the best play on words we had heard so far, and was embraced immediately.

Phil Vardy also turned out to be terrific at garnering publicity. Check out this from *The Sydney Morning Herald* of 16 March 1994:

SAILORS WHO WON'T BE HANDICAPPED OUT OF A RACE
By Garry Satherley

The mast man hasn't a leg to stand on. The navigator's a paraplegic. The skipper's dyslexic. They will be, you would have to say, the unlikeliest crew ever to set sail for Hobart in 50 Boxing Days. But among the 200-plus boats lining up for the start of the 50th Sydney–Hobart race next December will be the aptly named Carpe Diem *(Seize the Day), crewed by 12 disabled sailors.*

For Mr Phil Vardy, it will be more than just a yacht race. It is his dream that Carpe Diem's *performance in the Sydney–Hobart will lead to the inclusion of sailing in the 2000 Paralympics. And he hopes to raise $250,000 for research into childhood disabilities through a cents-per-nautical mile sponsorship scheme.*

'It's a way of putting something back,' the 45-year-old biologist said, referring to the fact that it was his disclosures that led to the disgrace and deregistration of Dr William McBride . . .

Last week, Mr Vardy resigned from his job as a biology lecturer at the University of Western Sydney to devote his time to the project. 'My main aim is to raise awareness of the abilities of the disabled,' he said. 'We want to show that it can be done and that it can be done competitively. I hope that from this will come a foundation concerned with sailing for the disabled. I hope some disabled kids might say: "Well, if these blokes can have a go, so can I." ' Sailors with disAbilities, as they call themselves, are seeking corporate sponsorship.

The skipper will be Carpe Diem's owner, Mr David Pescud, who, Mr Vardy says, is 'not physically disabled – but he's dyslexic; he has trouble with the tide tables'. Six other crew members are confirmed, with several possibles vying for places.

Six sailors were not enough. We needed many more than that to make up a viable ocean-racing team, so we pounced on every newsletter we could find, running articles saying that Sailors with disAbilities were looking for disabled people to race in the 1994 Sydney to Hobart yacht race. Every time someone rang, Phil would explain what we were up to, then invite them to come along to what were becoming regular weekly events, our Saturday morning Port Hacking sailing sessions. And come they did. They rocked up to meet the *Carpe Diem* in wheelchairs and with artificial limbs, some so unsteady on their feet they needed walking frames to hold themselves upright, or white sticks designed to let the world know they were blind.

Allan Grundy, who remains with the organisation to this day, roared up on his beloved 1947 Harley-Davidson motorcycle. Grundy had caught polio as a one-year-old. He used to have it from the waist down but by the time we met him, it was in the quads of his right leg and right calf muscle. He could not stand up without a calliper, and taking it off revealed a wasted little limb beneath. Never one to let the polio get in his way, he spotted a piece about us in the post-polio network newsletter (back then he believed, incorrectly, that he was getting post-polio symptoms), and thought to himself, why not?

As Grundy swung his leg off his Harley and swaggered up tough-guy style to the boat, he realised that he was not quite dressed for the ride. He was wearing his motorcycle gear, the classic Harley-Davidson outfit of cowboy boots, jeans and leather jacket, and there was no way I was letting those boots anywhere near my polished deck.

'They've got to come off, mate,' I told him, not realising that the calliper he uses to straighten his withered right leg was attached to the bottom of one of those specially made boots. 'Mate, there is one thing I know on God's green earth, and that is that you are not coming on here with those on. Get them off and do the best you can.'

Grundy took his boots off, which meant taking his calliper off, which made things difficult because he could no longer move around the boat. So he sat down on the boat with everyone else, cursing his inability to move around the deck. But once we motored out into the Harbour, put the sails up and let the *Carpe Diem* catch the wind, he started thinking, I like this. By the time we were back at our little mooring a few hours later, he was hooked – and determined to work out a way of making himself properly mobile on deck. He knew as well as we did that if he could not move around freely, he was going to be of no use to us.

Jeff Wilmott was a great find. Based in Warburton, Victoria, he was a transatlantic sailor with detached retinas. He had no vision in his right eye and less than 10 per cent in his left, making him legally blind. He was slim, good-looking, dark-haired, tall, well-educated, great sense of humour, considerate. His passion was music and he was rarely without an instrument, even if it was only one of the clay ocarinas he made and sold at the weekend St Kilda markets. Even as a musician, he had hidden talents.

'I'm a gumleaf player,' he let on one day.

'Naah,' we chorused.

'Oh yes,' he said, producing a gumleaf and silencing our disbelief completely with a tearingly beautiful rendition of *Amazing Grace*. The extraordinary, sweet sound bounced around the walls of our meeting room, sounding for all the world like a high-pitched fiddle.

'I told you so,' he said, when he finished.

Not all of the new recruits were rookies. Virginia Iliss – whose sister happened to spot an article about us – had already sailed extensively and was a skipper in her own right. At twenty, she had been diagnosed with myasthenia gravis, a neurological disorder that caused such weariness in Virginia's muscles that she could not support her own breathing or swallowing and was expected to die from the condition. After five bedridden years in a room set up like an intensive care ward at her parents' home, she changed her medication regime and started improving.

Virginia was slight but very experienced on the water. She was focused, feisty and utterly unable to resist the lure of the Sydney to Hobart, a race she had never attempted. She would become our principal navigator.

As each new crew member walked, crawled and stumbled on board, the need for sponsorship funds became more urgent. Who did we know who had money?

Computer specialist Harald Mirlieb approached his company, Com Tech Communications, for sponsorship. Mirlieb was turning out to be a gem, and not only because he already had years of sailing experience under his belt and was proactive in training other people. He may be deaf – he lost 90 per cent of his hearing after what he describes as a botched operation to counter an already existing hearing problem – but he is not backward about coming forward and he collared his boss in his usual forthright style, telling him: 'Look, there's a bunch of us trying to do the Sydney to Hobart, we're all disabled, it's the first time this has happened, are you interested in helping out?' They came up with about $30,000.

We're onto something here, I thought, and called Sharon Bond, a good friend of mine who worked with the high-tech company Aspect Computing. She collared her boss, CEO Pete Draney, and told him: 'I have this friend, he has this idea and he needs sponsorship. Would you mind if he came over and did a pitch, talked to you about it?' Pete Draney, to his eternal credit, agreed.

A pitch, though. Thanks, Sharon. It meant I had to turn up at Aspect's office in North Sydney with pieces of paper as though I knew what was on them. I memorised the spiel, something I had done a thousand times before but, boy, was I nervous. I didn't dare look at the no-nonsense businessman in front of me, with a tie on and his sleeves rolled up. I kept my eyes down on the paper as though I was reading from a pre-written script. It was not until months afterwards that he realised I could not have been.

'Thanks very much for seeing me. I should begin by telling you about Sailors with disAbilities – SWD. We are a group of people who have different disabilities who want to sail the Sydney to Hobart yacht race –'

'Done. How much?'

'Er, yeah, what we want to do is prove that just because we are what society calls disabled, we are not –'

'Done. How much?'

'Um, no, the thing is that I have got this boat and a group of us really feel that the time has come to make a point to the able-bodied world about just what people like us can really do when we are given a chance . . .'

Pete Draney stopped trying to interrupt. I carried on with my head down, 'reading' from my so-called pitch-script until I finally felt I had said enough. I put the papers down and looked at him.

'So what do you think?'

He sighed. 'I am sick of telling you. Done. How much?'

My mother, Joyce, and father, Reg, in the early days. He looks like he's just about to smile, and my dad had a smile so warm it got right inside you.

Me and my sister, Bronwyn. This was taken outside our family home in Caringbah when I was five and Bronnie was three.

Dad took this photo of me, aged ten, racing around Gymea near my grandmother's home.

Mr Jeffries, the teacher that made all the difference, and the class of 1J. I am sitting on Mr Jeffries' right.

Margaret and I on our wedding day – 8 February 1968. Note the groovy, late sixties going away outfits.

My daughters Gayle, in polkadots, and Katie, in the backyard of the Caringbah house Margaret and I shared. This was taken in 1977, when the girls were four and two.

Katie (far left) and Gayle were bridesmaids at my second wedding, to Susan, in 1988. We got married at Mum and Rex's house in Sylvania.

Mum and Rex at their farm in 2000. I love this picture – their love really has dignity and I think this photo shows it.

It's hard to describe the emotional impact that working with children has had on me. The safest way of looking after this boy, during one of the kids' days in Airlie Beach, was to keep him in my arms.

Kayle motoring out to sea on one of our wheelchair days.

Albert Lee in his element, on the
rail of the *Carpe Diem*.

Sharon Bond and Brian Scholtz
wring out Albert Lee's foam-filled
legs, after they fell over the side of
the *Carpe Diem* up in Queensland.

The 1998 Sydney to Hobart yacht race left me exhausted and my boat battered and bruised. You can see some of the damage on the left of the picture. That was the last Sydney to Hobart that the *Carpe Diem* ever did.

The crew for the 1998 Sydney to Hobart yacht race. From left to right, in the top row are Danny Kane, me, Grahame Clare and Kim Jaggar; in the middle are Harald Mirlieb, Michael Coles, Sharon Bond, Glenn 'Jack' Frost and Cathy Josling; then Sandy Collins and twelve-year-old Travis Foley; and in the front are Suzy Oram and Paul Borg. (*Courtesy Imagepoint Photographics Hobart*)

My mother christened my latest boat, *Kayle*, in July 2000 at the Cruising Yacht Club of Australia in Sydney's Rushcutters Bay.

Author Helen O'Neill and I, after the book I never thought would exist was finished.

'Um . . . $25,000?'

The man didn't bat an eyelid. He just said, 'Fine. Sign me up.'

'Right. Thanks.' I couldn't believe my ears.

'One tip, though,' said the man in the suit.

'Yes?'

'Stop being such a rabbiter.'

Draney later let on that he had decided to say yes the moment I walked through his office door, before I even opened my mouth. He had interviewed so many people for jobs over the years that he could smell which ones meant what they said when they walked in the door. Even before he shook my hand, he said he knew what I was like, that I could and would make a difference. I totally fooled him that I could read, though.

The only payoff our two new sponsors wanted was that we badge the *Carpe Diem* with their names. We agreed to display Aspect's name and logo on our hull and sails for what's called the Northern Campaign – a series of races and regattas that take place during August between Sydney and Hamilton Island in Queensland's tropical Whitsundays. Com Tech's name would appear on the boat for the '94 Hobart itself. I honestly don't think they really felt that they were going to kick a goal by backing us, but if we somehow managed to score some television coverage, their companies would get some lovely exposure.

By Easter the money was sitting securely in SWD's bank account. We invited our sponsors down to meet the team. Pete Draney, a man who can't understand why anyone with half a brain would step off perfectly good terra firma – he thinks it is worse than jumping out of an aeroplane – was up at the dockside meeting the team. He watched one man hobble up the walkway on aluminium half-crutches and thought to himself, I guess he must have polio.

The man shimmied his way up onto the boat and disappeared down below as Draney watched him. Then the crewman came back up again. Without any legs. Draney's eyes nearly popped out of his head. The crew-man turned around, spotted his audience, and called over to Draney: 'Never go down below. Look what happens.' Draney didn't know whether to laugh or cry.

With the sponsorship money in the bank, training had to begin in earnest. And, boy, did these guys need training. I thought about the team we had so far – they were paraplegic, deaf, blind, amputeed, with everything from Parkinson's disease to heart trouble and cancer. Some of the new recruits had ocean experience, but most of this motley crew had never even sailed before. Somehow, in just nine months, we had to turn out twelve highly honed, perfectly drilled, race-fit individuals who would be able to handle anything the Sydney to Hobart could throw at them. This crew had to know the *Carpe Diem* inside out. The sighted sailors had to be able to jib, tack and trim the boat with their eyes closed. Those who were visually impaired had to be so well trained they could do their job standing on one leg in a force 10 gale.

We had a basic problem with the boat in that the *Carpe Diem* was not built for disabled sailors. It was narrow across the centre and there were winches and all sorts of other pieces of equipment everywhere making it hard for paraplegics, in particular, to bum their way around the vessel when it was still, let alone in churning, white-water ocean conditions. Until I watched my crew-mates trying to negotiate this environment I had never even thought about, it really had never occurred to me that people with limited mobility would have problems moving around my vessel.

Too bad. We did not have time to remodel the boat. They were going to have to learn how to navigate about the *Carpe Diem* as quickly and efficiently as any able-bodied sailor because when you take a boat out onto the ocean, anything can happen. Even a good day can be truly violent, like being in a washing machine as the vessel rises and falls by metres every few seconds. With able-bodied people the rule is: 'One hand for you, one hand for the boat.' Some of my new team didn't have two arms, and those with no legs – or legs they couldn't feel, let alone manoeuvre – were going to have to learn to do all the tasks expected of any trained crewman on an international-standard yacht race.

Ocean racing is dangerous. However well prepared you are, you never know what you will hit once you are out beyond the easy reach of dry land. As the skipper, these souls were my responsibility. Where the hell was I going to start?

Our first serious training run was an overnight sail from Yowie Bay, where the boat was still moored despite our efforts to find somewhere more wheelchair-friendly.

The plan was to navigate our way out of the Port Hacking waterways and head south as we hit the ocean, travelling parallel with the Illawarra coast past Wollongong, Shellharbour, Kiama and the Seven Mile Beach National Park before reaching the more sheltered waters of Jervis Bay. Then we would turn around, retrace our steps, and head north of Manly and Dee Why to Pittwater before we turned back and came home. The round trip is about 160 miles and, winds permitting, should not take longer than twelve hours there and twelve hours back. No worries, mate, I told myself grimly.

On the morning of truth I woke up with a start at around 6 am. I did what I always do when I'm living on my own. I grabbed my wet weather gear, kissed the dog goodbye and walked out the door of my Grays Point home. Like many old salts, I have a pre-ocean routine, and that morning I stuck to it to the letter. I took a quick drive into town to pick up the provisions that I always take sailing – a stick of salami, cheese, olives, a loaf of bread, some ground coffee and the newspaper (one of the great days of my life was when I worked out how to find the long-range weather report). Then I met up with Rob Sealey. He was my insurance policy. Rob is a mate from way back. He is a top sailor: level-headed, experienced and a very steady hand. I knew if the worst came to the worst and things went badly wrong out there on the ocean, he and I could sail the *Carpe Diem* back to safety on our own.

So I was nervous, but the nerves were contained as we picked up the *Carpe Diem* from my place and motored it around to a jetty where people could drive cars almost down to the mooring. All they had to do once they had parked was negotiate a few shallow steps and they could get onto the boat. That was deliberate. A mistake I had already made was organising for some would-be members of SWD to come and have a look at the boat when it was moored beneath what might as well have been about 40,000 stairs. That was a terrible day for wheelies and non-wheelies alike. Those who could walk picked people up, and we did manage, but I realised for the first time that being picked up can be a very confronting experience emotionally for some people, and that anyone doing it has to be aware of that. If the disabled can't even do that for the disabled, that is a bit of an indictment. So, the fewer steps, the better.

That day it was May and it was cold. The boat was ready to go – I had made sure of that – but the weather was overcast, with a thick, heavy cloudbank hanging ominously above the bay.

'Tell you what, David, we are going to sort them out on this trip,' said Rob, looking out to where a wind was whipping itself into a frenzy. We sat and waited for everyone to turn up. I coiled ropes, then I uncoiled them again. Rob started drumming his fingers. What on earth was keeping them?

My mobile phone rang: a call telling me that one of the paraplegics could not make it. I was furious. The guy concerned was a good sailor and we needed him on board. What I did not find out until long after the trip was that I had stuffed up. His personal hygiene routine took him so long each morning that he simply could not be with us before 9.30 am. The poor man had been too embarrassed to tell me what the problem was and I was too inexperienced to anticipate it, or to ask. We never saw him again.

Before I had time to obsess too much about his sudden no-show, Rob and I heard a clattering from the other side of the mooring. Everyone was appearing at once, and from the amount of luggage and the sheer number of well-wishers coming our way, it looked like our crew thought they were emigrating to the Bahamas. The wheelchairs we were expecting, and the wives and husbands, but not the great-aunts, the long-lost uncles and every friend they had made since primary school. Our crew included the full gamut that day – paraplegics, deaf people, the blind, one-armed and one-legged – and they had hot water bottles, guitars, sheet music, hats, blankets, bottles and so much food the bloody boat was in danger of sinking just from the weight of it.

There were suitcases bursting to the seams with clothes, as though these people were sailing away for six months, not just one brief night. 'Bring wet weather gear,' I had told them without seeing the need to elaborate. What a fool. They had brought everything waterproof they could lay their hands on – I even seem to recall spotting a golfing umbrella amid the luggage – but nothing that would qualify as what I understood sensible wet weather gear to be.

'Oh my God,' Rob Sealey muttered quietly to me. 'You have got to be kidding.' He rolled his eyes in utter disbelief, understanding that he didn't need to say anything more.

What he and I knew, but I had stupidly failed to explain to everyone else, was that when you have sailed a lot you really strip yourself down. You have the very best clothes but the absolute minimum: thermals, good quality woollen gear, Gore-Tex. The ideal kit is light, compact, easy to stow and easy to move. Put twelve people on a boat, even a 54-footer like the *Carpe Diem*, and there is no room for anything else. Take those twelve people out into race conditions and there will not be time to fall over twelve mountains of luggage looking for that one thing you desperately need but cannot find. Rob and I knew that. These guys had to learn it. Watching them dump more and more stuff on the deck, I had no idea if my new crew thought they were going to go deep-sea diving or climbing Mount Everest, but they had brought everything just in case.

Rob shrugged his shoulders, stood up, and started quite literally pushing things downstairs with a crowbar. I shook myself out of my stupor. It was clearly not just the crew who were wet behind the ears and about to get a shock to the system. Their supposedly experienced skipper was as well.

We untied our moorings and let the lines go to the strains of a farewell so intense it would not have surprised me to see monks blessing the water we were floating on as everybody waved their goodbyes and we motored the *Carpe Diem* off down the Port Hacking channel towards the South Pacific Ocean. As the boat moved past Jibbon Beach, the last stretch of sand before we hit the ocean, the wind started to freshen up and we lifted the mainsail, shooting the *Carpe Diem* out wide to pick up a bit of current. The sea was starting to become a little bit bumpy out there with a swell of one to two metres. The crew were looking anxious but not too green and as Rob helped adjust the sails, I recall saying to him that if things carried on like this, we shouldn't have too much trouble getting out to Jervis Bay at all.

Then, of course, the wind picked up, turning what had been cold, damp conditions into sheer wet misery as freezing salt-spray began shearing over the bow of the boat. Uh-oh. These guys were not ready for it, they were certainly not dressed for it, and they could not have been more miserable. As the wind laid into us at about 30 knots, which is not too bad by ocean standards but certainly makes things very uncomfortable, the *Carpe Diem* began to get really thumped, and before you could say 'Er, you did all take some seasickness pills before we set out, didn't you?', my intrepid crew started feeling seriously seasick. I can't remember who was the first to throw up but once one of them had shown the way, a stream of others turned green and started spewing.

Now, I have a rule that you cannot chuck up below deck on my boats – or if you do, you clear it up so quickly that I never see it – the reason being that if it gets loose downstairs it permeates the boat and you can smell it wherever you go. It is absolutely disgusting. The crew had taken this on board but it was not as easy as it sounded. Vomiting above deck could also end in tears, though. A few weeks before this fateful trip, on a day sail up to Pittwater, Albert Lee – a double amputee who stored his state-of-the-art mechanical legs below decks when he was sailing – had managed to projectile vomit upwind for close to five metres. It was a remarkable feat and something I had never seen anyone manage, but it was sadly overshadowed by the fact that, at the time, the entire crew was up on the rail, using their weight to try to keep the boat as flat as possible while it was racing through the water. Albert's technicolour yawn hit every single one of them and started a chain reaction that no one wanted to see repeated.

'Nothing ventured, nothing gained,' I muttered to Rob Sealey as more and more of our comrades turned green and disappeared below deck. We passed Helensburgh, Fairy Meadow and the big smoke of Wollongong. Then a sou'wester hit us, and things got even nastier.

I started watching the group dynamics at play. It was wet, though it wasn't raining, and while people were getting horribly cold they were refusing to take advice. I would tell someone if they sat in a certain spot they would get wet but rather than moving up to the high side when there was a wave on its way – which would have helped the boat's passage through the water as well – bravado would take over and they'd tell me, 'No, I'll be alright,' only to have the wave come through and leave them soaked to the skin with no second set of clothes and no dry towel.

To make the Sydney to Hobart yacht race work, I would have to sail this boat very differently, I started to realise. I would need to give people a lot more time. Up until then, I had been convinced that we could race the boat through that event. Watching the projectile vomiting going on all around me, it was clear that was not going to happen. We were going to have to passage the *Carpe Diem* through the hazardous course, starting with the rest of the racers at 1300 hours on Boxing Day in Sydney, and finishing whenever we finished.

There were a few crewmates who were weathering the conditions and proving themselves quite useful. But those who were having trouble were either hurling into the white water or hiding away downstairs, getting very, very cold.

Had Rob Sealey and I been manning the *Carpe Diem* on our own, we would have had a great time zipping across the water that day. We would have hoisted whatever sails were best suited to the conditions and sat back to enjoy the ride. If we had been alone, the boat would have been neat and tidy, with everything where it should be. As it was, we and the handful of other able sailors were tripping over clothing, bags, water bottles and people lying all over the boat in different states of disrepair. I was busy trying to work out who would be able to sail with me: who of the sick sailors might come good, and what they would be able to manage on the boat.

In the middle of all this at least one person was getting so wet and cold they were in danger of becoming hypothermic, which meant that I didn't have Rob on the rail any more. He was downstairs, rolling the sick sailor into a sleeping bag, and making sure that they were going to be okay.

We made it to Jervis Bay at about eleven o'clock that evening. It was dark, cold, wet and horrible. Most of the crew were huddled away in the dank recesses downstairs, where there was a horrible smell of vomit, and someone had blocked the loo, so that wasn't working. I was not happy.

I sat up on deck to get away from the hideous smell, ate a few olives and watched Rob steering.

'Straight back home, Dave?' he asked.

'Reckon so,' I said, spitting an olive pip out into the sea.

We turned the boat around and headed north, back up to Port Hacking and home. It was getting light and everyone was tired now, some of them semi-comatose downstairs. I went down, had a look at the sorry mess, made two cups of coffee and grabbed some salami, cheese and bread.

As I poked my head back up and looked at Rob, he just said: 'Shit, Dave. What have we done?'

There were a few guys winding, trimming and doing their best. When I asked Albert Lee to do a headsail change, he bounced his legless body up to the front of the boat with Harald Mirlieb and Brian Scholtz, who had a history of heart problems and had undergone bypass surgery in 1988. Both Mirlieb and Scholtz were proving they would rarely succumb to seasickness. The problem was that most of those who were not ill were caring for those who were, leaving hardly anybody to look after the boat. TX was not how a Sydney–Hobart crew performed.

'This is not going to happen,' I told Rob as we pushed past Port Hacking towards Bondi Beach. The crew were getting very weak and a few of them seemed to be dancing around the edge of hypothermia. 'Forget Pittwater,' I said. 'We've got to get these guys out of this.'

'Absolutely,' he replied. 'Right now.'

It was ironic, really. The boat was bursting at the seams with food – exactly what these people needed – and we were telling them, 'Eat something, put something, anything, in your stomach.'

'No, no, no,' came the chorus of agonised groans as they rolled back over in their bunks.

The torture had lasted around eighteen hours, and as we neared the protective Heads of Sydney Harbour, the weather started turning once more. The southerly eased a little bit, down to about 20 knots, as we tacked our way between the Heads and went around to Watsons Bay, picking up a mooring where we could sit the boat down in the soft, placid water.

Within half an hour the sun came out and it turned into a lovely, sparkling day. The boat dried out and one by one faces started appearing from below decks. Green turned back to pink and our would-be champion ocean-racing crew perked up completely. They brought food out from the hole, cranked up the kettle to make some hot drinks, and started singing and telling jokes to each other.

Suddenly I was hearing 'Wow, that wasn't too bad'

and 'Hey, we can do this'. 'Let's go to Pittwater.' Rob and I were both knackered from working all night. We did not want to go anywhere. I remember thinking, it's going to take more than a bit of sunshine, my friends. We are never going to get to Hobart.

Well, I was wrong. Disabled people are tough, they hang in there. They have to. Not one of the crew members on that boat dropped out because of that first, sorry sail. No one even batted an eyelid. The thing that impressed me was their absolute grit. As we motored the boat back into Port Hacking, I could see people mulling over what had happened; their expectations, their performances and what they needed to do to get up to speed. A change of attitude began blowing through and the committed, focused, determined individuals they had been as we left Port Hacking returned. A bit of seasickness and a touch of hypothermia were not going to slow these guys down. They were going to get to Hobart.

I tried to think about that as I cleaned my stinking boat up afterwards and got ready for the next training run. It went better. Things really picked up when Birkenhead Shopping Centre, which has a marina with no steps, offered us a berth for free. A mooring where we could actually get disabled sailors onto the boat without any major dramas was a godsend. It meant the serious training could begin. A club in Sydney took us on and got us racing with them; only short training races around Sydney Harbour, but they were exactly what we needed.

More crew members appeared. Phil Vardy met a paraplegic, Vinny Lauwers, during a trip to Melbourne.

Vinny was remarkable. He had been sailing since he was twelve and had always loved the water, but on 7 January 1990 – a date that burned its way into his brain – he broke his back in a motorcycle accident when a car came straight through a stop sign, knocking him off.

He snapped his spine at T7 and became a paraplegic, destined to spend the rest of his life in a wheelchair. But Vinny was not the kind of character to let something like that put him out of action. The accident also resulted in short-term memory loss, causing him to forget almost everything he knew about sailing. When Phil met him, Vinny was doing a series of sailing courses, his aim – although it took him a while to tell us this – being to sail around the world single-handed. He was already working on the design of the boat that would take him.

Vinny wanted to do the Sydney to Hobart yacht race to get ocean miles and experience. He asked me to keep it to myself, so I did, and he told me, 'Look, I want you to teach me as much as you can.' When I heard his plan, I thought, yes, that's possible – if it's Vinny trying it. Disability is a state of mind, and from the word go it was clear Vinny had the kind of mind that made him possessed by his goals. He was going to either do it, or die doing it. You can have a long life or you can have a good life seemed to be his attitude, take your pick.

Vinny would drive up from Melbourne to train with us at weekends, often sleeping in his four-wheel drive overnight and being the first one, apart from myself, at the *Carpe Diem* come Saturday morning. There he and

I would talk over his plans for the design of the boat, and the trip itself.

Everyone had different reasons for being on the *Carpe Diem*, but my task remained clear. For this to work, I had to turn myself into the skipper of this crew. Being master of a boat is a hell of a responsibility at the best of times, but we were trying to do something one step beyond what anyone else had ever attempted. Safety-wise, this was really tricky stuff.

I worked out a series of drills. We had to be able to abandon ship fast, which meant that everybody, paraplegic or otherwise, had to be able to move about the boat quickly and easily. We had life-rafts packed away down below and it was imperative for the crew to be able to get one of those on deck in five seconds flat. I figured if it takes us five seconds to do that, it should take us five seconds to get anyone on deck, whether they could walk or not. Blind, deaf, armless, legless or paraplegic, whatever you were doing, anywhere on the boat, you had to be able to get on deck in five seconds. We drilled in Sydney Harbour; we drilled in the ocean.

It was hardest on the paraplegics, but I had to tell them, 'If you can't manage it, you can't come. It is going to have to be as simple as that.' It took a lot of practice. Vinny's upper body strength was already very good because he was doing a lot of wheelchair road-racing. He and the other wheelies, such as Matt Speakman, who also lost the use of his legs after his motorbike collided with a car, spent a lot of time at the marina trying to figure out how to do it, and after a few weeks of drilling they were flying around the boat like gorillas. Before too long, they could all do it.

We watched for what could go wrong. My intention was not to lose anybody or compromise safety in any way at all. Gradually we settled on a set of rules for the *Carpe Diem*, some of which would become safety benchmarks after the disastrous 1998 Sydney to Hobart yacht race in which six sailors perished and another fifty-five had to be rescued from the huge seas. On board the *Carpe Diem*, whenever we were in ocean water, everybody above deck had to wear their safety gear. We developed a standing rule that if the wind hit 25 knots, everybody above deck would hook themselves up to the boat with their safety harness. At night, as soon as the sun went down, everybody hooked up as well. And if someone felt like hooking up at any other time, they should.

We gave each sailor a bumbag containing things such as emergency whistles so they would have a better chance of being found if they fell overboard, and we started doing what felt to the crew like endless 'man overboard' drills in the ocean as well as the quieter, contained waters of Sydney Harbour. I never let on who was going to go over, or when. Emergency drills like that are not much use if everybody is expecting them. Harald Mirlieb was usually the fall guy, although Rob Sealey would jump into the breach when required, and while people did not enjoy those sessions, everybody saw the need for them.

As the training went on, we tried to work out what people's strengths were – their abilities as opposed to their disabilities, which started to disappear as they spent more time on the boat. Sure, you tended to avoid the coffee that Richard Bowler sometimes made – he had Parkinson's disease and shook so much he would only use lukewarm water and you'd invariably only get half a cupful of that by the time he had handed it over. But those with strong upper bodies, such as the wheelchair guys Matt and Vinny, were terrific grinders – a job involving turning the winches that pull the sails about the boat.

One of the big-muscle jobs on the boat is lifting the sails up in the air. Watching them coast up the mast might look fairly effortless to the uninitiated but the mast of the *Carpe Diem* was 57 feet 6 inches in the air – the height of a six-storey building. The mainsail on weight weighs 50 kilos, so what Matt and Vinny were doing was like hefting a 50 kilo bag of cement onto their shoulders and lifting it up a six-storey building. Those jobs are all about immense shoulder and arm strength and once those two were hooked into position in the middle of the boat, they ceased to be disabled.

John Woodward, who had destroyed his foot in a shooting accident when he was fifteen, had been sailing for five years by the time he set the other foot on the *Carpe Diem*. Known as Woodie, he moved about so well on his prosthesis you would never have known he was missing a limb.

Blind Jeff Wilmott memorised the entire layout of the boat, from every nook in the bow to each cranny on the foredeck, so he would know where everything was.

This gave him a terrific advantage at night. When everyone else was stumbling about in the semi-darkness, Jeff could confidently lay his hands on anything. He ended up being most comfortable preparing food and looking after everything below decks, but we did try him out as what we call the 'strings man', the one who looks after the ropes, because at night he could tell by feeling the pressure in each rope which one needed taking up.

One thing we had to talk about was what might happen if somebody died out at sea. Brian Scholtz had a heart condition and he warned us that if he did have a heart attack, and he might, our options were limited. 'If I become unconscious you might have to give mouth to mouth, perish the thought,' he said. 'But if we are at sea and in a race you must keep going. If I croak, you will probably want to get rid of the body as quickly as possible, so you may have to call a helicopter. Beyond that, there is nothing anyone will be able to do.'

Elsewhere, disabilities were turning out to be abilities. Take Albert Lee, who had fallen off a Sydney train one night back in 1982 and lost both legs above the knee. Many such amputees never learn to walk again but Albert, a very goal-oriented individual, was determined to finish his training as an optometrist on his artificial feet. He never considered keeping his prosthetic legs on once he was on board – they were nowhere near stable enough for him to balance on the moving deck – and because his stumps were uneven, he never attempted to 'walk' on them. Instead he skirted around the boat using arms strengthened by wheelchair racing and basketball.

He could catapult himself through little gaps most people would have to crouch into to make their way through. Able-bodied people have to duck beneath the boom, the horizontal beam that holds the mainsail in place. To Albert it was an open door. And his centre of gravity was so low, he was very unlikely to come off the boat.

Albert was missing his legs but he had all of his stomach and back muscles intact, while the paraplegics, such as Matt and Vinny, were dragging the dead weight of their legs around with the added disadvantage that half of their chests were not working, making it ten times more difficult for them to move around the boat than an able-bodied person. Albert had full use of his stomach and back muscles and no dead weight at all, so he could move around the boat like a little monkey, zipping on decks from downstairs in a split second. No challenge was too great. As scared as he might have been, and he did openly admit to it, he would always take on the task at hand.

Al Grundy found himself watching Albert's awesome agility almost jealously, thinking it might not be so bad to be a double amputee. 'The thing is,' Grundy would then admit, 'as soon as we got back and I watched him put his legs back on, I realise it wasn't such a good idea.'

Harald Mirlieb was also an asset; he was a big, strong, fit guy in his forties who had already done some sailing at one of the Sydney yacht clubs and he fitted in beautifully as another big grinder and winch bloke. Harald insisted on trying to use his hearing aids. Almost totally deaf without them, he could hear to an extent with them, so he would wrap them up in Gladwrap to keep them dry before sticking them in his ears. It didn't work – they would get wet and konk out anyway. Even so, his deafness didn't turn out to be too much of a problem, because most of the time sailors can't hear one another anyway – the wind and boat speed won't allow it. But knowing Harald's condition, if I needed to tell him something and he was at the front of the boat, I would tell the guy next to me, who would tap the guy next to him, until someone would tap Harald, who would then turn and look at me. If I wanted to lift the headsail up, I'd point at Harald, point at the headsail and give the wind-up sign and off he'd go.

As I worked with Harald I realised that deafness is very much like dyslexia because it makes its sufferer removed and remote. Harald misses a lot of the nuances of life, just as I do. He misses them because he never hears them; I miss them because the words everyone else reads in a flash – the signs one encounters driving up a highway, for example – will never speak to me. I learnt to love sailing with him. He is such a powerful, strong, robust character, and someone who wants people to be content. When he's drunk he sings German drinking songs and somehow he manages to do it in tune. Above all else, he kept the others happy.

Every time we went out I was getting to know my crew better. On the ocean one day we were sitting on the deck, blazing along in the breeze, discussing what stuck in our minds that related to our disabilities. Matt

Speakman's answer came in the form of a story about what happened after the motorbike accident that left him in a spinal unit for days on end.

'I'd been in there for months,' he told me as the wind filled the sails and we tore along the clear, calm water. 'And do you know what? The best day I had ever had in my life after that accident was the day when they sat me in my wheelchair and took me outside. I had been in air-conditioning for months and feeling the breeze on my face was amazing.' He smiled at me.

'Do you know what the worst day of my life was?'

I shook my head.

'That came ten minutes later. One of the nurses was wheeling me along, and another nurse coming the other way said to her, "Where does he have to go?" I wasn't a real person any more. I had turned into my wheelchair.'

As the crew fitted ever more perfectly together, we sailed and trained, sailed and trained. We tore around trying to get the *Carpe Diem* thoroughly transformed from a simple cruising vessel to a reasonably sophisticated racing boat. We were training every Saturday, bringing new people on board and working out how to winnow them down into the twelve-strong crew we needed. I used to tell everybody, 'I want you here at nine o'clock,' and even just saying that sorted out some of the wheat from the chaff.

Three of the crew lived in Melbourne and used to travel up to Sydney every week for training. Jeff would sleep on the overnight train he caught on Friday night at

Flinders Street station in Melbourne, arrive at Birkenhead Point at 8 am, sail with us all day Saturday, and
take the overnighter back to Melbourne in time to sell
ocarinas, little clay flutes that he makes and sells at the
weekend markets. Other people would rock on up at
half past nine from just around the corner, saying, 'Aw,
sorry, I couldn't park the car.'

Those who didn't know much about sailing soaked up
more and more information from those who did. As
Al Grundy put it: 'We were all disabled. We knew this
was a good thing and we wanted it to work. There was
animosity but there was a real jelling too. Because we
were all in the same boat.'

We worked out our strategy. We needed racing miles
and ocean experience, which meant jumping on board
the Northern Campaign, a series of races up the coast
of New South Wales and Queensland that work as a
training ground for the big one at the end of the year. As
well as a stream of smaller races, this would take in the
Mooloolaba to Airlie Beach race, the Hamilton Island
Regatta – a wonderful week-long event in the blissful
waters of the Whitsunday Islands – and the Gosford to
Lord Howe Ocean Race. We needed that last race
because it is a Category One, like the Sydney to Hobart
race – offshore all the way. If we turned up to the Sydney
to Hobart having done a Category One, it would make
it that much harder for them to stop us. But none of this
meant anything if we couldn't get into the Sydney to
Southport, and that's where the fun really began.

We put in our entry for the Sydney to Southport race,

a three-dayer if the conditions are right, in good time. The cheque cleared, the forms went through. It was to be our first ocean race and a real test. All was well.

Then, nothing. From where I was sitting it looked like simply entering was causing huge headaches for the race organisers because no one had ever had to deal with a crew like us before. They didn't know whether to let us compete, what the ramifications would be if they did decide to do it. I assume they took legal advice. They didn't want to let us do it. There was quite a lot of talk bouncing around the general sailing community about a boatful of cripples not being able to do an ocean race. I only ever heard it second-hand. No one said this to my face but comments such as 'They don't know what they're doing' were flying about.

The organisers put us through the hoops. We did three safety inspections where they come and check all your equipment. There is a certain level of equipment you have to have, life-jackets, your radios, your maps, lights, torches, buckets, the steering has to be right . . . We had to have an annual inspection, and there were sometimes spot checks back then, so they gave us two of these as well, all within a month, the head safety officer going over the boat with a fine-tooth comb. The boat was very safe, so no problems.

But the days ticked past and still there was no answer. 'It's like this,' I told the crew. 'The Sydney to Southport is the first in our run-up races to the Sydney to Hobart yacht race on December 26. It's a three-day event and a pretty tough one. It's run by the Cruising Yacht Club of

Australia, the heavyweight Sydney-based sailing club that also organises the Sydney to Hobart, so we need to get our entry accepted by them. The thing is, I don't think they want us to race.

'I don't know about you but as far as I'm concerned we are going whether they let us race with the fleet or not. They have accepted our cheque, they have been over the boat with a fine-tooth comb. Ten seconds after they tell us we can't compete in this race, we are going to hit the phones and have every TV camera, every photographer, every newspaper journalist down here on the boat and we are going to talk to them.

'We are going to run their race whether they like it or not. We will go out five minutes before the gun goes off and I will sail the *Carpe Diem* across their start line. We will complete the Sydney to Southport.

'Agreed?'

They agreed. As Al Grundy later said, 'We were going anyway. The question was, were we going with the race fleet, or going on our own in a blaze of publicity the CYC would regret for years to come?'

The race was due to start on a Saturday. A week before the event I had still heard nothing. The days ticked by. Sunday . . . Monday . . . Tuesday . . . Were they going to say yes or no? Were they going to say anything at all?

By Wednesday I was ropeable and ready to call the journalists I had primed to be ready at a moment's notice. The race organisers were stuck between a rock and a hard place – the ramifications for them were potentially enormous – but there was no way I was going to budge.

At eight-thirty on Wednesday night my mobile rang. It was one of the organisers, finally with an answer for us.

'David,' he said, 'well done. You have made it. Good luck in the race.'

Oh Jesus. We were in.

9

ON THE MORNING OF the Sydney to Southport race the crew were suited and booted in shiny new wet weather gear. They looked the part from the tops of their carefully combed heads to the tips of their immaculately clean fingernails. It was their first offshore race – as far as we knew it was the first offshore race any disabled crew had ever done – and the crew were ready for the 380-plus nautical mile coastal passage from Sydney to Southport, on Queensland's Gold Coast. But they were nervous as all hell.

They had polished their kits and brushed their eyes and every one of them was on board and ready, as requested, by 9.30 am. As we waved goodbye to the assembled well-wishers from Birkenhead Marina and sailed off to the start line in Sydney Harbour, there was very little talking going on.

Boat races typically begin with a series of gun and flag signals. First comes the preparatory ten-minute warning, at which point most skippers will set their watches. Then the five-minute gun goes, where they check their watches again and confirm the time. Then comes the one-minute warning. Then, go. All the racing vessels set off together. We were tacking back and forward in the Harbour, waiting for the starter's one o'clock gun to go off, when Matt Speakman, who had become legendary on board for his sense of humour, suddenly piped up: 'Skipper, it's bust. The starboard winch has bust.'

'That's not funny, mate,' I shot back. 'Don't tell me that ten minutes before the start of a race.'

'I'm not kidding,' he said. 'It's real, it's broken.'

'*What?*'

'Really. I'm serious. It's fucked.'

Now, there are a dozen winches on the boat, and they control everything – all the sheets, all the halyards. Anything that has any pressure on it goes through a winch but the two that do most of the work are those primary ones. I shook my head and left it, not really believing him. We had already worked flat out to fix a radio problem that had threatened to take us out of the race entirely, and now this. Even if Matt was right, we wouldn't know the extent of the damage until we attempted to change tack. If what he said was true, we would not be able to, because we would have no way of bringing in the headsail.

The start line was a jostle with sixty-four other boats, so I stayed out of their way. As the starter's gun echoed across the sparkling water, we gave the rest of the field a ten-minute lead and headed out on a port tack towards the Heads and the wide blue South Pacific Ocean. Even then I did not really believe Matt, but once we had made our way outside the Heads we had to catch the wind and travel north, and that meant changing tack to starboard.

Matt was absolutely right – that winch had sheared clean through. I quickly thought it over. No primary winch was serious. It meant we could only go in one direction. Not a good look on a major ocean race. But if we pulled out of that Southport race, it would have been the end of our sailing program and we could kiss the 1994 Sydney to Hobart goodbye. So I did what any responsible skipper with a boat of no-legged, one-armed sailors on their first ever ocean yacht race would do. I said, 'I don't care, we're going. Let's jerry-rig it.'

We cross-sheeted it, took the sheet so it went around that broken winch to the only working primary on board, which would have to do the work of both until we hit the Gold Coast and our final destination of Southport. Thus bandaged up, the boat started racing up the coast, past Newcastle and Port Macquarie. The wind was behind us and the *Carpe Diem* was moving quickly and relatively comfortably, despite being hobbled. Dusk fell.

At 10 pm in the starlit darkness, a big surly blow came through and hit us hard. Up to 60 knots of wind slammed straight at us out of the south-west, bringing four-metre waves in its wake – not enormous but enough to create a huge amount of noise and vibration. The entire *Carpe Diem* started rattling hard and it was all we could do to stop the shaking and clip the boat to calm it down, because that shaking breaks things. Some of the big boats were already suffering with dismasted vessels and broken equipment. We struggled on, painfully slowly.

We had to reduce the sails because there was no way we could take another injury that might put us out of this race, but even that proved a nightmare. All the batons broke and they went through the laser disc, and I couldn't get the mainsail down. Richard was driving and Rob and I were standing there with torches, trying to work out how to get the damn thing out of the way. Richard jibbed the boat and somehow it broke through and the whole mainsail tumbled onto the deck.

The boat was awash downstairs. The seals in the bow had broken loose and were leaking, so every time we hit a wave it was like Niagara Falls coming in through the front of the boat. Downstairs everything was soaked and the entire crew were freezing. Al Grundy and the rest were doing their utmost to keep to the regulations we had set up about where you could take off your wet weather gear to minimise dampness, but they were soaking anyway. Vinny tried to hold himself upright with one arm as he struggled to get his clothes on and off with the other, while the boat thrashed backwards and forwards over the waves. Poor Phil Vardy, who was nauseous but unable to make his way above deck in time to throw up overboard, threw up in one of his personal effects bags, thus containing the damage. Grundy, who bore witness to the event as he lay on the galley floor feeling gruesome, later said he thought it was an incredibly gutsy thing to do.

I gritted my teeth and tried to sail out of there. When you get a big blow like that you just put it up your backside – that's a technical term in nautical circles – and run with it. We could have ended up in Fiji.

It was all over by 8 or 9 am. That next morning we took stock of the damage. A lot of ropes were gone, and there was broken gear – one of the maxis had broken a boom. So while we had been wounded we were still in the race. We stitched up our wounds as best we could and limped our way north toward the Gold Coast over the next three days. The sun came right out, which brightened everybody, but then the wind dropped off so much that I could not get us past Australia's most easterly point of Cape Byron. I kept tacking one way and then another, until finally the wind picked up slightly and pulled us back up towards Tweed Heads.

I was tired. I had catnapped in the cockpit but I had not been below deck at all over the three-day race. I was forcing myself to stay awake, surviving on lollies and caffeine to make sure everything was okay. Finally we spotted Point Danger, which meant only 20 miles to go, and everyone started bucking up. We crossed the line, sliding down the breakwater into the beach just as the sun was coming up again. All twelve of us just sat there looking at each other. We knew what we had done but we didn't understand it yet. 'We are here,' someone said, in disbelief. Yes, we had finished, but we were all still grappling with what it meant.

It had not been an easy race. We had been smacked about and the boat had about six feet of surf sloshing around downstairs. There were tools floating about, and electrical panels under water. I saw water in places I had never seen it before. Everything was soaked through, from the carpets and cushions to Harald Mirlieb's earpiece and the foam in Albert Lee's expensive prosthetic legs. Amazingly the electrics – including the radio and the GPS – all kept working.

We pulled everything wet upstairs, hosed it with fresh water and laid it out on the deck. The warm sun was beating down on us, bleeding heat back into our bones, when Brian Scholtz came over to me and said: 'That was a great race, wasn't it?'

I just thought, geez, Scholtzy. Oh bugger. And I felt tears begin to prick away behind my eyes. It had been a hard race but we had done it. We'd come in just about last, but all twelve of us were walking on the moon. I'd had the helm when we crossed the line and my nervous tension was such that as the boat crossed it, floods of tears started streaming down my face so fast I could barely wipe them away.

I had crossed many lines before but emotionally that was the toughest race I have ever done and nothing I've done since has even come close to it. It was the first big test of the crew and while we had a long way to go before we would be ready for the Sydney to Hobart, we had already done what had never been done before. We had picked up Mount Everest and moved it a couple of miles to the right. Had anything gone wrong, those race organisers would have hung me out to dry. As we went over the finishing line all I could think was, thank Christ.

Then I said, 'Right. Get these sails down.'

The battery was flat so we could not start up the engine and motor into Southport proper, but as we finally got it going and slid past the point, I felt a tremendous feeling of relief, release and achievement. Yes, we had done it. I looked around at the guys and saw faces reflecting the elation hitting me. No one had the words to express it. Someone handed out beer and biscuits and the back-slapping began. This was the first ocean race ever done by a disabled crew in the world, as far as we knew. It was certainly the first in Australia.

There were banks of TV cameras and press photographers waiting for us as we motored into the marina. Matt, Phil and I did most of the talking, though the odd journalist collared Al Grundy too. He told them that we could do anything now. 'We are all just looking forward to going to Hobart at the end of the year,' he said. 'This was the first major hurdle. Now we have done it, nothing will get in our way.'

In front of the cameras the *Carpe Diem* crew was a united front. Behind the scenes it was a different story. I was a hard, harsh skipper with a tendency to blow up at people rather than sit down and explain things fifty times. From the start Al Grundy put my temper down to pent-up anger caused by my dyslexia, although rationalising it can't always have made it easier to deal with.

Even so, as he will happily admit, he was fairly stroppy at times and started bucking my authority long before the Sydney–Southport. I found myself screaming at him to do things and he would yell back: 'I'll do things for you, mate, but all you've got to do is ask me. If you scream at me, I'll not do it, or I will do it but slowly.'

Everyone from Matt to Virginia ended up on the wrong side of my tongue as I wrestled with a fury that seemed to well up from nowhere and was often completely out of proportion to the issue at hand. A big frustration was asking people if they knew how to do things, hearing them say 'Yes', then putting them to the test, only to watch them fail.

'If you can't do it, don't say you can,' I would explode at them with a passion I can only liken to the footie field, where people find themselves punching out their best mates in the heat of the moment. I am told I even threatened to punch people out on the boat, though I certainly never did, and as soon as we stepped off the boat, all was forgiven. It takes a determined person to sit through that kind of punishment, but everyone on this crew was utterly resolved to get to the Sydney to Hobart.

The thing is, when I go to sea my arse is way out there. I do not want to kill anyone, I can't afford for anyone to die, so I train them to do it right, over and over again, and over and over again people will do it wrong. I have no patience with that kind of thing and I only knew one way of saying to people: 'If you don't put your life-jacket back where you found it, and this boat sinks and you need to get your life-jacket in a hurry, you are going to die. It will all be over red rover, pull the blanket up, turn the lights off, you will be dead, because you didn't put the fucking life-jacket back where you were supposed to.' How many times should you have to say it?

It was not always about safety issues. I had handcrafted the *Carpe Diem* so that my wife and I could sail around the oceans of the world, and the interior had beautiful cedar panelling. I hated it when people put their feet up on it. I would say it once, say it twice, say it three times, and then explode: 'What don't you understand about "Don't put your feet on the furniture? Get. Them. Off".'

Different people dealt with it in different ways. Harald, of course, was deaf, and would often be present when I found myself yelling at people for some misdemeanour or other, losing my cool so badly I would start ranting and raving. The crew would be sitting on the boat, dead quiet, waiting for the storm to be over. All except Harald, who would lean against the railing and look out to sea with a big smile on his face. The bugger had turned off his hearing aid.

Phil Vardy and I disagreed at every turn. If he wanted to do things one way, I would invariably want to do them another and the longer we continued, the clearer it became that ultimately something would have to give. I don't believe you can have two skippers on a boat, and when it is my boat, and I have thousands more sea hours under my belt, I should be the skipper.

Things came to a head as we kept training and racing, entering the Mooloolaba to Airlie Beach offshore yacht race in Queensland because we needed to rack up some more distance in the sea and at 510 nautical miles it offered just that. If we attempted to enter the Sydney–Hobart having only done the Sydney–Southport we would be seriously looked at.

Then Phil Vardy and two other SWD members decided that they wanted to take part in the World Disabled Sailing Championship in the UK. It would be the first time an Australian team would compete and it paved the way for one of Phil's wider goals, linking Australian disabled sailing to the rest of the world. He would later say it led indirectly to a series of personal and national firsts for both Vardy and disabled sailing in Australia.

But competing in the UK meant these sailors would temporarily drop out of our team. I wasn't happy. I thought we needed to keep our sights set firmly on the Sydney to Hobart, and I made it clear that if they were going to go, they could be putting their crew places in jeopardy. There was competition for every spot on board the *Carpe Diem* – by that time we were juggling about eighteen people who wanted to go on the twelve-man race.

Phil went to the UK anyway.

Back on the boat, we carried on racing. In the Mooloolaba to Airlie Beach race we were beginning to jell as a team, and everyone was becoming more used to their positions on the boat. The only person who had any qualms about competing was Jeff Wilmott, whose attendance meant he would miss the national gumleaf playing championships he had been trying to win since the eighties. He thought about it, briefly, then phoned the organisers up, made his excuses, and wished the other competitors the best of luck. He needn't have worried too much. In 1997, he would go on to become the joint winner of the event. He would finally win the title outright in 2001, with a rendition of *The Three-penny Opera*.

During the Mooloolaba to Airlie Beach race, we were racing well. But sailing is like that, you never know when things are about to go spectacularly wrong. At about 3 am on day two of what would be a three day race we found ourselves doing one of the most dangerous manoeuvres in sailing, an involuntary Chinese jib.

Now, there are two ways of turning a boat. You can tack it, putting the bows of the boat through the wind. Or you can jib it, putting the quarters or stern of the boat through the wind instead. Jibbing itself refers to changing from one jib to another; from port to starboard or vice versa. Normally when you jib, you haul the main boom in to the centreline of the boat and let it out on the other side. A Chinese jib, which usually happens through lack of concentration from the helmsman, occurs when the boom goes round in a full 180 degree arc and hits the other side – crash – leaving the main boom on the same side as the spinnaker pole. The spinnaker is left flapping wildly because it is exposed fully to the wind. That is really, really bad. Everything is wrong. Sails are flapping, things are going bang, spinnaker poles are bending. The whole boat is totally out of control. It puts an enormous strain on the entire boat, and when you are sailing, the main aim is to try to keep all loads off it.

What you do *not* want in these circumstances is for it to be 3 am, coal-dark and with a high wind – which was exactly our situation.

One lapse and the boat Chinesed. Albert Lee got hit

hard in the head as the boom spun across the deck with no warning. Luckily he was tethered on and was only thrown as far as the rail.

I grabbed the helm and started fighting for control. The spinnaker disappeared, torn into tatters. I was screaming for Rob Sealey to 'Get on deck. Get up front,' but he was nowhere to be seen. He moves like a cat around the deck and I needed him here *now* to help me sort out this crisis.

'Where is Rob?' I yelled at the nearest crewman.

'I don't know,' came the reply.

'*What do you mean you don't know? Find him!*'

We were screaming through the water now, totally out of control, doing 12, 14 knots. It was impossible to hear anything through the noise.

A head appeared from below deck: 'He's not in his bunk, skipper.'

Shit, he must be overboard. Somebody, tell me he isn't overboard.

'*Find him! Is he up front?*'

'I can't see him,' the crewman called back.

So far only the spinnaker had blown up – the entire boom could have shattered, but thankfully we had been spared that. I struggled with the helm until the boat was back on the other jib and under control. I kept shouting through the wind, 'Where's Sealey? Find Rob Sealey!'

Al Grundy came down from the front of the boat.

'Have you seen Rob Sealey?' I screeched at him.

'I think he's up the front,' said Al.

'Go up there,' I yelled. 'You go and find him. Tell him I want to see him.'

Two minutes later Rob came wandering down from the front of the boat with a grin on his face. 'Yeah, boss?' he said, as though nothing at all had happened. 'What do you want?'

Thank God. I thought I had lost him for good.

Not long afterwards we found ourselves up in the Whitsunday Islands, doing the Hamilton Island Regatta. It is a fantastic week of sailing, not least because it marks the end of a racing patch that had taken us from the cold of Sydney's July to Queensland's September tropics. The week was tricky for our navigator, Virginia, because it was her job to make sure we avoided all those coral atolls sticking out of the reef. We had a lot of gear breakage and we came in last. But we finished.

In typical Whitsundays style, the competition is highly social, so it should have come as no surprise to me to be woken up by Jeff at three o'clock one morning. I was sleeping on the boat, deep in the arms of Morpheus, when I heard his voice.

'David, get up. There's a woman I want you to meet.'

'Mate, piss off,' I said.

'Nah, come on,' he persisted. 'Get up. She's a woman. And she makes documentaries.'

I stumbled out in my underpants and climbed up on deck. Sure enough, there was a woman there, with a big smile on her face.

She grinned at me. 'We've been playing snooker,' she declared proudly.

Playing snooker? I thought. Jeffrey is as blind as a bat. What is going on?'

'Do you mind if I ask you something?' she said.

'Oh no, you go right ahead,' I said, gritting my teeth. This was going to be good.

'I come from a company called Locations Tasmania, and we want to make a documentary about you. The thing is, I've never heard about anything like you lot, this is going be amazing and I'll tell you exactly why. What we'll do is –'

'Fantastic,' I cut in. 'Great idea. Wonderful. Super. Brilliant. I know, let's have a cup of coffee and talk it through tomorrow.'

She and Jeff sat there, motionless.

'Now, go away.'

I crawled back into my bunk and woke up the following morning vaguely remembering this weird conversation about a woman and a documentary. Jeff was in a bunk opposite.

'Mate,' I called across to him, 'do you remember something about some sheila and a documentary?'

'Yes,' he said. 'I think so. I need some coffee.'

We pulled on our shorts and headed above deck, and there's this woman, the same one from my dream, sitting on my boat with a mug of coffee in her hand, talking a thousand miles an hour and full of plans.

We listened to it all and said, 'Yes, great. When we get back to Sydney,' thinking it was never going to happen. But when we got back to home port, we did get a phone call. Not only did Locations Tasmania want to make this documentary, they wanted to pay us into the bargain.

Training days turned into filming days as the crew

polished themselves and stood under the spotlight answering questions such as 'What do you expect to get out of this race?' and 'Do you really think you can do it?'

We did session after session of filming, one of which took place on a beautiful, classically sunny Sydney afternoon when we took the *Carpe Diem* out to the Heads and into the ocean. The plan was to do a jib. There were two cameramen on the boat, shooting our one-leg-below-the-knee amputee John Woodward as he stood on deck and handled the ropes, and another in a frog suit in the ocean ahead of us, ready to film the bow of the boat as it ran towards and over him. Yet another cameraman was in a chase boat to get pictures of us pulling away after the manoeuvre, although there wasn't a lot of breeze out there.

The jib began and all was going smoothly. John was standing on deck as the boom moved across and the boat started taking the wind in her sail. Suddenly a rope got coiled around John's prosthetic leg. It took up the weight and whipped the leg off, leaving John shocked but still somehow upright. The prosthesis flew up high above the mast, doing circle after slow, lazy circle as we watched in stunned silence. It was just about to hit the water when Al Grundy called out: 'Bit of a man overboard.'

I went mental. I stormed up to the director and said, 'You must never release that footage, ever. If you let the CYC see that they will never let us near any race – never! Let the CYC see that and we'll have Buckley's chance of getting into any race ever. They won't want anything to do with us. Tell me you're going to destroy that. Tell me!'

By the time the frogman in the water had crawled out to let us know that he had never seen anything so strange, we were all wetting ourselves with laughter. My threats must have done the trick. It never did get used in the documentary, that footage. Or leggage, I should say.

We kept drilling, whether the cameras were on us or not. The training program was difficult because we had people who had never sailed before, some who had varying levels of experience, some who thought they could when they couldn't, and some who were very good and quick. It was all part of the normal problematic process of building a new crew, but compounded by disabilities. Sometimes people had the wrong disability. Matt Speakman and Vinny Lauwers were proving to be terrific sailors. I would have loved them to have been blind or deaf so they could move around the boat, but they couldn't.

Vinny, in particular, was outstanding. He was a remarkable athlete, and a very quick sailor with an excellent personality for the ocean. It was no surprise to any of us when he managed to become the first paraplegic to sail around the world, alone and unassisted, in 2000.

Albert Lee was good but still learning what his limitations were. He could not make coffee for us when the boat was at 45 degrees, for example, because without his legs much of the world was above his head. That's the short of it, pardon the pun. The legs themselves were busy becoming what you might call a standing joke. He never wore shorts back then – it would take him several more years to 'come out', as he describes it, as an obviously amputeed man – so his prosthetic legs were always dressed in long trousers and shoes. Taking the legs off meant taking the lot off, and it was not unusual for a sleep-befuddled sailor to come off watch, see what looked like someone lying in their bunk, and grumpily find themselves somewhere else to sleep. When they woke up and looked around properly, they would invariably find the culprit was Albert's legs.

Al Grundy had to build a new carbon fibre calliper because the salt water was rusting his steel one right through. His boots had a bolt that went into the bottom of his shoe, and the calliper sat on that, so Al had his carbon calliper fitted inside his deck shoes so he could grip onto the floor of the boat with the sole of his shoe when the *Carpe Diem* was racing on its side at 45 degrees.

Jeff Wilmott moved to the galley to look after the rest of the crew downstairs. He was good at it. He did get seasick but he just dealt with it down there, and he created a world for himself where he knew where everything was. He could make you a banana sandwich in the dark without having to think twice.

But there was a lot more going on than just learning where everything was, and how to change headsails or steer the boat. We were learning how to operate together. If a paraplegic was working on deck and he needed something downstairs when the weather changed – blockout, sunglasses, a jumper – people had to automatically start offering and asking. We were having to learn that those who can have got to, and those who can't have got to ask, be gracious, and be patient.

Most of the crew had now done the Southport and the Mooloolaba to Airlie Beach race. They were starting to feel good about themselves and the fact that they could sail together and put up with each other's vomit and smelly underpants. The camaraderie that had begun to build in the *Carpe Diem* team from the Sydney–Southport race was really beginning to tighten. They were becoming a well-oiled machine, and in a race like the Sydney to Hobart you need that kind of glue. One morning as we were racing down the waves and I was watching Vinny Lauwers steering, with an ease that showed it was becoming second nature to him, I found myself thinking, yes, they were genuinely becoming a team. Even so, the crew had not shown any real toughness yet. They had not been truly tested.

The last race we had to do before the Hobart was the Gosford to Lord Howe Island run, which sees yachts from clubs across the country compete in a 408 nautical mile race north across the Tasman Sea. The race is unusual because of its exclusivity – Lord Howe Island's World Heritage listing means that only a certain number of yachts and crew can visit the island at any one time. And importantly for us, it was Category One all the way – a true ocean race. There are only two such races in Australia which run from New South Wales across the open seas to an offshore island. The other is the Sydney to Hobart, making the Gosford to Lord Howe a vital training race for would-be Hobart crews. It was run by the Gosford Sailing Club – well out of the reaches of the CYC – who accepted our entry without even a quibble, so away we went.

We had to pick the crew for Lord Howe and it was obvious that the Lord Howe team would be the Sydney–Hobart team. I gave the SWD crew selection committee a list of names, which included Phil Vardy, and said: 'Pick anyone on that list, I'll be happy with that.' When the crew list came back to me, Phil Vardy's name was not on it.

The race itself was tough but relatively uneventful. Bringing the *Carpe Diem* home was a whole different ball game. We came out of Lord Howe with a good forecast: the weather boffins were predicting nor'westers of 20 knots for three days, followed by a bit of a sou'west front, flicking to the south-east. Fine, I thought, 400 miles at 20 knots. We'll be home in three and a half days.

That delivery run, as such voyages are known, was peopled by myself, Sharon Bond, Harald Mirlieb, Brian Scholtz, Richard Bowler, Virginia Iliss and Harald's wife, Terje. We sailed from Lord Howe with another boat belonging to Keith, a friend of mine: two sister ships travelling home together in a fleet of around twelve other boats that had all raced their hearts out a few days earlier.

Over in the west there was a lot of weather action visible in the darkening sky as lightning streaked down into the edge of Australia. I wasn't entirely happy about that and we had also seen a forecast for local storms. Keith was running five or six miles northside of us, so I rang him up over the radio system and asked him what he could see.

'My barometer's going up, mate,' came the crackle over the radio. 'Yes, I'm watching it. I'm not too worried, though. You don't get bad weather on a high.'

We radioed off and thought no more about it.

The *Carpe Diem* was hammering along, doing 13 knots right on course, so I took a look around – Richard was helming beautifully and there were clear skies with nothing untoward happening, so I went downstairs where everyone else was and started plotting a position on the chart.

As I climbed back upstairs and across the deck to relieve Richard on the helm, a 70 knot westerly front hit us with no warning at all, like a truck on a highway. The headsail disappeared, torn to ribbons and out of control. Before you could snap your fingers the mainsail was out of control, too. The battens – fibreglass rods running across the back of the sail to give it shape and support – were torn out of position in such a way that the sail was jammed onto the mast, and the boat was at the mercy of the wind tearing through that sail. There was no time to lose. I had to get it down to regain control of the *Carpe Diem* or we were all in very grave danger.

The next twenty minutes were the closest I have ever come to dying at sea. It was night – pitch-black. I was on deck, everyone else but Richard was downstairs. There was no time to call anybody.

The mainsail was damaged – torn and shaking the boat, which was trembling under the enormous vibrations of the wind slicing through it. Left like that it would tear the centre out of the *Carpe Diem* by ripping the mast right out of the boat's middle. Getting the sails down would stabilise the boat. Then we could make plans about setting up storm sails and dealing with the conditions. Every second I wasted brought us closer to disaster.

I let loose one of the ropes, which should have dropped the mainsail straight down on deck. It didn't. The sail was stuck and, in the dark, I could not see why. What I did not realise was that the battens had been driven forward in such a way that the only solution was to cut the sail down. I fought the wind and staggered forward to the mast to slice through the problem. The mainsail fell down, but it fell into the water and began dragging the boat down. I had to pull it up onto the boom so we could lash it out of the way.

So I lay over the boom, pulling the sail back up onto the deck. It was tough work. The wind was so strong that spume from the ocean was travelling along the horizontal. Every time I turned my face, the water felt like it was slicing into it because it was coming so hard. Then – with no warning at all – we jibbed. One minute my feet were on top of the boat and I had the boom under my belly, the next the boom was flying out into space with me hanging over the top of it.

Worse still, the sail that I was lying on was sliding out from under me into the deep, black water, so I was frantically pulling on it while trying to stay on top of the boom. When I looked down, all I could see was violent ribbons of white froth snaking across the deadly sea beneath me. The wind was so strong, I could barely breathe. Oh Jesus, I thought, I'm in trouble now. All of this had happened so quickly I had not even thought to put my safety harness on. Stupid, stupid, stupid. I remember thinking, this could be it. This could be the day you die.

I was furiously trying to work out what I could do. My options were limited. I was literally hanging out over the side of the boat with no way of getting back in. I was probably only about eight feet away but in a wind like that, and in the dark, it might as well have been eight miles. The sail was sliding, the boom was disappearing off into the water all the time and it was all I could do to keep frantically scrambling to stay balanced before my grip gave way completely. Then the boat jibbed again, throwing the boom in the other direction. Unbelievably, I was flung back onto the deck of the boat.

The boat was lurching about so badly that everyone downstairs knew there was a major problem. Harald came on deck and the two of us crawled onto the foredeck and fought through the driving wind to sort out the headsail, finally getting it lashed down so it was not flogging the boat about. By this stage the boat was lying on its ear – very, very dangerous. Normally the bow of the boat cuts through the waves. We were so out of control that we were staggering into them with the side of the boat, which meant every single wave was crashing right over the top of us.

We hoisted the small stormstay sails, they took the load and we coaxed the boat back under control. Slowly, the *Carpe Diem* started doing just three and a half knots, maybe four. The crisis had taken about an hour out of my night, and ten years off my life.

For the next three days we battled big winds of up to 70 knots, and the problem then was that in the she-mozzle with the mainsail, we had lost the running backstay on the starboard side. Losing our starboard running backstay but still having the port one meant we had to stay on port tack – the only way we could go was to Brisbane, more or less. In those conditions that is not the end of the earth – all you want to do is get some-where and sort out the damage – but even so, Sydney was a better option.

The following morning Virginia did one of the bravest things I have ever seen in my life. The sea was big. The *Carpe Diem* was rising and crashing through a 10 metre swell, and there was almost 50 knots of wind around. The mast was flicking violently through 40 degrees. If we were going to make it back to Sydney we had to get the starboard running backstay clipped back into its slot.

Virginia was the lightest person on board, therefore she would be the quickest to lift up there and the quickest to get back down. She is a strong, gutsy lady and an experienced sailor, but she was still compara-tively frail and she had never done that before. But when I said to her, 'Virginia, I've got a job for you,' she just cocked her head to one side, looked at me and without a second thought said 'Yup' and disappeared below deck to get ready. Unbeknown to us, she then swigged about half a bottle of the homeopathic concoction Rescue Remedy to fortify her nerves for what lay ahead. I steered the boat while Harald, who is a big, strong bloke, got ready to lift her up on the halyard.

Virginia poked her head above deck and said, 'What if I hit my head?'

I had not really thought about it so I just shrugged. She ducked below again and re-emerged with a tea towel, which she wrapped around her skull. God, she looked ridiculous.

She shimmied up about 15 metres of the mast, which was whipping about in the wind in a terrifying fashion, and she was hanging on like a koala to a tree. She took up a cable that she had to hook onto the mast, a hard thing for her to do as her condition makes lifting her arms above her head very difficult indeed. I could see her summoning up the energy from somewhere – one, two, three, then she somehow did it, scooting back down to the relative safety of the deck as soon as her work was done.

Harald and I couldn't help ourselves. We looked at her, looked at the tea towel, and started giggling so much we nearly wet ourselves.

A few hours later, while the wind was still gusting at over 50 knots, I went downstairs to get something and spotted Virginia with her head in the toilet cleaning everything while all hell was still blowing upstairs. She really is a remarkable sailor.

That year they stopped the Sydney to Wollongong MS bike ride for the first time in the event's thirteen year history. On land, gales caused millions of dollars worth of damage, blacking out around 60,000 homes across New South Wales, fanning bushfires, tearing roofs off houses and resulting in the death of a woman riding pillion on a motorbike which was blown into the path of an oncoming car. Scores of other people were injured. We were 350 miles out in the Tasman Sea and the whole boat got covered in red dust that had come off the mainland. It could barely have been more dangerous.

When we got back to Sydney I reconsidered things. I was the most experienced person on board and if anything happened to me during the Sydney to Hobart, it could spell disaster for the crew. Up until then the idea was that everybody but me would be physically disabled. Now I realised that I could not risk sailing without another experienced able-bodied sailor, and Rob Sealey was not available for the race. With only eight weeks to go, I had to make a big decision. I phoned my good friend Al Cooper, who was living in Canberra.

'I've got a favour to ask,' I said, cutting to the chase. 'Would you be prepared to sail the Sydney to Hobart?'

'Tell me more,' he said.

'The crew I am sailing with is not quite like other crews. Everyone bar you and me is physically disabled.'

'Aaah . . .' he replied. 'Tell me more.'

I outlined who we all were and what we were trying to do. He would come on board as a helmsman and watchmaster, which meant splitting up the twelve people on board into two teams which would work on three-hour shifts, one to be run by him, the other by me. Al had no offshore racing experience apart from sailing the Gosford to Lord Howe Island race back in the mid-eighties, but I knew what he was capable of.

'There's one other thing you should know,' I added. 'There may be resistance from some of the crew members. The whole point of what we are doing is taking the first ever disabled crew on the Sydney to Hobart. You may meet people who do not want you on board because you are able-bodied. But I need you, in case I fall over the side, so I am going to push for this even if it does cause trouble. What do you think?'

Silence.

'Yes,' he said finally. 'I'll do it. How do you want to introduce me to the rest of the crew?'

We did that on a test sail a few Saturdays later. As the *Carpe Diem* motored out from Drummoyne towards the Sydney Harbour Bridge, Al turned to the assembled sailors and made a very difficult speech.

'I am embarrassed to be here,' he said. 'I know I do not represent what you want to represent, and I will understand if some of you resent my presence, but I agree with David that this is a prudent thing to do. As David has told you, I have industrial deafness from working as a fitter and welder years ago. I am not using that as an excuse to get on the boat but just to point out that when you speak to me, look at me. And I will look at you.'

That seemed to settle everybody down. 'I think you've won them,' I told Al quietly as the wind filled the sails and the *Carpe Diem* started moving.

The crew was complete. Finally we were ready. The next big thing was Hobart.

10

WITH THE SYDNEY TO HOBART race came publicity. No one had ever seen a crew like us and it seemed as though the whole world wanted a piece of it.

Everybody on board the *Carpe Diem* was disabled in some way. Our sail trimmer Harald Mirlieb was legally deaf, our bowman Albert Lee was a double above-the-knee amputee. Matt Speakman, the headsail trimmer, and Vinny Lauwers, who ran the port primary winch, were paraplegics who spent their land-based lives in wheelchairs, and found the freedom of sailing enormously liberating. Vinny would tell people it made him feel human again. His love of the sea was already becoming so great that he was having a 40-foot yacht built that would become his new home.

Jeff Wilmott, our cook who ran the mainsheet on the second watch, was blind. Brian Scholtz, the strings man, ran all the ropes on the boat that controlled the fine adjustments of the sails. He had suffered ongoing health problems as a result of his heart condition. Downstairs, Virginia Iliss, a skipper in her own right despite suffering a neurological disorder, was our principal navigator and looked after everything below decks on the *Carpe Diem*. Richard Bowler, our sail trimmer, was diagnosed with Parkinson's disease in 1990, and although he had sailed since he was a child, his condition impaired his ability to react to things effectively. Allan Grundy, the mastman, contracted polio as an infant and had one withered and practically useless leg. John Woodward, the foredeck man and spinnaker trimmer, had only one foot. Even helmsman Alan Cooper, our token able-bodied sailor and my much-needed back-up, suffered from industrial deafness.

What bound us together, though, was not what we could not do. It was what we believed we could. We, a bunch of cripples, were about to compete against some of the most experienced crews in the world across 630 nautical miles of the roughest and most dangerous seas on the planet. The Sydney to Hobart is one of the highest profile and toughest ocean races ever devised. It boasts uncertain weather and high drama, and attracts more international media coverage than almost any other yachting event, bar the Whitbread Round the World Race and the America's Cup.

And this year was special: it was the fiftieth anniversary of the race's beginnings back on December 26, 1945, when nine yachts first sailed the course. Alongside us, 370 other boats would be jostling to get out of Sydney Harbour, amid hype and hoopla unlike anything seen before. The huge turnout was not only a record fleet for the Sydney to Hobart, it was the biggest ever to contest any ocean race. The media were having a field day, and the newspaper, television and radio journalists who came anywhere near us heard nothing but calm, solid confidence.

Behind our brave words, we were well aware that things were not going to be easy. We had agreed to keep filming during the race for the Locations Tasmania documentary still being made. Every morning, a helicopter would find us and pick up the footage Virginia and Matt had shot over the previous 24 hours – an added complication in a course that had the potential not only to be exciting but bloody dangerous. The chopper belonged to the ABC, who were also involved in the documentary and would screen it first, before it went onto endless rotation on cable.

I talked the talk and made sure the crew were aware of exactly what we might be up against. What not all of them knew was that despite all my wise words, I had never finished a Sydney–Hobart race. My two previous attempts, both times as a crew member on other people's boats, had ended prematurely after equipment failure. I really wanted this one.

The boat was moored at Birkenhead Marina. There may have been frantic scenes taking place at the CYC in Rushcutters Bay where most of the other race boats were moored, but here it was very quiet with just one other

boat and crew getting ready for the big event. At about
8 am, I took stock of my feelings. Nervous, yes, but confident. It might have been Boxing Day but I did not feel
overly bloated. I had picked at the previous evening's
Christmas dinner with all the trimmings at my mother's
house while the rest of my family tucked in, and I had
drunk virtually nothing. The last thing you need on the
morning of a big race is to feel seedy.

Before too long the rest of the crew started appearing.
Each had brought a single small bag – we were learning
how little racers needed with each passing competition.
The rest of our stuff would be waiting for us in Hobart.

The pre-race weather briefing held two days earlier
had given little cause for alarm but in this race it is
only in Sydney Harbour and Hobart's Derwent River
that you can predict reasonably calm conditions.
Potentially the worst patch was going to be Bass Strait,
where the currents, wave patterns and shallow water
could make the seas very, very cruel.

As we got ourselves ready, Phil Vardy appeared. He
had come along to see us off from Birkenhead Marina on
his boat. We knew that he was bitterly disappointed not
to be racing with us, so that was a very nice gesture. The
Carpe Diem motored out towards the start line under
the overcast sky. We started tacking to and fro, waiting
for the gun that would release the first fleet of old-style,
wooden boats – a break from race protocol to mark the
Sydney to Hobart's fiftieth anniversary. Yachts of every
shape and size were readying themselves for the off,
from the antique-looking vessels to the state-of-the-art,

multimillion-dollar, one-off fibreglass creations that were practically designed to fly. Across the length and breadth of Sydney Harbour all you could see from the green hills on one side to the green hills on the other was a big row of colours as the other 370 boats jostled about. The crews looked beautiful in uniforms of sponsored hats, shorts and tops, and some were resplendent in Hawaiian shirts, although they were about to travel in the wrong direction entirely for that kind of weather.

On board the *Carpe Diem* we were already rugged up in our matching white Com Tech T-shirts and red wet-weather gear. Even that was not quite as it seemed. Each wet weather outfit was especially modified for its crew member depending on how many arms and legs they had. Those without legs, or with legs that didn't work, would have to spend their time bumming about the boat, so their gear had extra padding in the backside.

Beyond the boat, the scene was all so beautiful that my toes started tingling. That did not mean we wanted to be stuck in the middle of it. It was so crowded that boats were in danger of knocking into each other, and the last thing we needed was for a pre-race collision to take us out of the Sydney–Hobart before it had even started.

'Christ,' said Alan, 'we'd better get out of here pretty quick.'

'You're not wrong, mate,' I replied.

The shot of the first starter's gun rang out – the signal that the old timber boats and big fast boats should get under way. By the time our huge group was allowed past the line it was hard to move because all the other sails were taking the wind. We jostled through a fairly narrow gate and limped on what wind we could muster towards the Heads, and the ocean. I didn't know what to expect but I knew the crew were tough, so I figured once we had the wind in our sails, we would be okay.

Outside Sydney Harbour the Pacific Ocean's swell meant that everybody had to find their sea legs. There was a southerly blowing, so on that first day, after we turned and went through the Heads to start the long journey south, it was a fairly bumpy ride. We were beating through the headwind, slapping into that sou'easter until long after night fell. It was hard work, and bumpy, travelling south along the New South Wales coastline. That night was wet and cold. Many of the crew were seasick and getting tired, but we were up among the first third of the racers and running very well.

The following morning the off-watch crew rolled out of their bunks to a lull. We were moving towards Bass Strait, a stretch of water which separates mainland Australia from its island state of Tasmania, and one of the most unpredictable patches of ocean on the planet in terms of the wind, tide, current and shallow water. It was a beautiful ride across flat, clear seas under a perfect blue sky with just enough wind, about 20 knots of a northerly blow, to make it feel very easy.

A big sou'wester was forecast so I nudged the *Carpe Diem* towards Flinders Island, which lies north of Tasmania's north-eastern tip, just in case things started getting rough.

'Mate,' sang out Al Grundy from the front of the boat, 'Bob Marley is alive and kicking.'

We all looked over to see what he was pointing at. Lodged along the length of an otherwise clear blue sky was a huge roll of a cloud that looked to Grundy like the biggest joint he had ever seen. We all knew that under that cloud bank, which was four or five hours away from us, lay the business end of town.

It was late in the afternoon so we cranked up the sheets and prepared for the storm that lay ahead. We later discovered that some other boats bailed out of the race at that point because they didn't think they were up to it. I had no intention of bailing out of anything. I dug our heels in and used the wind to race across Bass Strait before the weather had a chance to hit us. Strategically we had set ourselves for the gale that was coming by using the good weather to sail into the west of the gale's front, in the hope that when it hit we could go off at an angle and use it to push up to the east coast of Tasmania. We were racing hard, so we needed to keep our largest sails up until the moment the gale hit us, and then ready the boat for the heavy weather very, very fast.

It was night, and Al Cooper was helming when it finally reached us. The crew sped up to match the conditions, got the spinnaker down and changed the sails superbly, with only minutes to spare.

But when the gale hit, the boat became an animal, a bolting horse. Despite our prudent rigging we were doing nine knots in ever roughening seas. The noise was incredible as the rigging shook and the sea slapped into the side of the *Carpe Diem*.

The wind went up to 50 knots and the boat started tossing so violently that Albert Lee, the bowman, was disappearing completely under metres of foam which were flooding the deck every time we hit a wave. When the foam drained off, he would shake himself a little and carry on with what he was doing. Whoever is on the helm has some control over how the bowman is treated and while Al Cooper was still up there, he put the boat severely through a big wave. 'Albert's going to get you,' I told him. But the weather was taking its toll. Al Cooper, who rarely gets seasick, started suffering to the point where he was hallucinating, seeing people in the cockpit with him that not only were not there but that should not even have been on the *Carpe Diem* at all.

Downstairs it was mayhem. Almost everybody was getting sick. Al Grundy, one of the few who did not, had got into the habit of barely eating anything when he was racing, and put it down to a problem with the food. Whatever the reason, things were not good. I popped my head above deck through the hatch about an hour after the gale set in.

'You've got to slow the boat down, guys. I've got people down here sick and they're not going to make it,' I yelled over the noise of the howling wind. Someone had fallen and hurt themselves and the boat was keeled over so badly that those trying to sleep were struggling even to keep themselves inside their bunks.

The guys on the deck weren't too happy about cutting

knots off our speed but they did, and once the boat slowed down to about six knots, everything became much steadier. Even so, it was a long, nasty night. When Al Cooper's hallucinations got the better of him and he finally realised he couldn't continue any longer and asked for someone to relieve him, he could not believe how bad the humid stench of vomit was below decks.

As things calmed down the next morning, we were scooting along the east coast of Tasmania very competitively indeed. Then I made a fatal mistake and headed close to St Helens Point, just south of the Bay of Fires. Before we left an old friend had told me, 'Whatever you do, don't go anywhere near St Helens.' Stupidly, I took the *Carpe Diem* too close and parked right under a wind shadow. We had been battered around the night before and were a little bit disorientated, so we were half enjoying the quietness when I thought, oh no, we're becalmed.

The wind was up in the mountains and the landmass stopped it from coming anywhere near us. I spotted a boat further east on the horizon, grabbed the binoculars and realised it was charging along. That was where we needed to be but there was no bloody wind to get us out there.

We struggled to get out of the landmass's grip, all the time watching a procession of boats that had been behind us following the rocks around and having no trouble at all. From racing well, we were dropping back, and it was all because of my not very clever strategy. To my eternal shame, I have to say it took us six hours to escape. We inched the boat out slowly, limping painfully away from the mountainous lull. Finally we picked up the wind, but we had lost our place in the pack.

By early the next morning we were skirting around what we call the organ pipes, a massive, stunning tessellated formation of rock columns at Cape Raoul, near the bottom of Tasmania. Just as we passed it a huge pod of hundreds of dolphins found us and started cavorting through the swell all around the boat. Suddenly they were all around us, accelerating past, dropping back, leaping out of the sea with an effortless exhilaration. Because of the size of the waves they were looking down at us out of the water in the early morning light. I had never seen anything like it.

We finally made it into the shelter of the Derwent River. We were about to become the 130th boat to finish the 1994 Sydney to Hobart yacht race. Of the 371 boats which had begun the race four days earlier, only 309 had made it to Hobart. We were not in the top third – much as we wished we were – but at the end of the day that was not really the point. We had done it. As far as we knew, we were the first disabled crew ever to compete in a major ocean race and had earned our place as just another team in the world of able-bodied people – ABs as we called them. Six months earlier that had not been the case.

I turned around to the crew and said, 'Who wants to bring her over the finish line?'

Vinny Lauwers didn't say anything, he just looked away, later explaining, 'I did not want to be taken off the winch and what I was doing. I had sailed bloody hard to get here. I just wanted to finish my job and get over the line.'

I think Richard Bowler steered us across in the end,

and making our way across the final hurdle was a joyous moment on the boat, which rang with the noises of happy people shouting out yippees and yee-haws that eclipsed everything. Everybody had a different reason for taking part in the race. All Vinny wanted to do was get off the boat and go home, because he had realised that he had the skills to start his own campaign. Even so, for him, as for each one of us, this was a dream realised.

We had cameras chasing us on boats and hand-held cameras in our hands, doing interviews with journalists and each other for the Locations Tasmania documentary as we sailed the boat wherever the news crews wanted us to go.

Somebody, Matt or Vinny I think, turned around and said to the rest of us, 'Guys, we have severely kicked AB butt.' And the whoopees rang out some more.

We motored in to the marina to meet friends and family, and yet more media, of course. As we docked the boat and people readied themselves for dry land, reality reappeared in the form of prosthetic legs that had been tucked below deck, and wheelchairs that had been flown down to Hobart to meet us. On board, this crew were in their element and utterly without the disabilities that defined them on dry land. Watching them climb back into the appendages that defined them to so many people was very sobering indeed.

The race had taken a huge toll. The crew were soaking wet, freezing cold and very, very tired. Al Grundy, for one, had no intention of ever going through anything like that again.

We got off the boat and dealt with the press. I found myself saying to one journalist, 'If we look at ourselves we find things other people can do better than us. Does that make us disabled or does that make us people?'

Then we all disappeared off into the crowds to have a couple of beers and some proper food. The next morning, memories of the pain and drama were already receding into the distant past. The more we ate and drank, the more human we felt, and before I could stop myself I was saying, 'So, guys, what about next year?'

'Aaah . . .' came the slow, hesitant replies. 'Yeah. Why not?'

The *Carpe Diem* did enter the Sydney to Hobart the following year, with some of its original crew members and a smattering of new ones, and this time our entry was accepted by the race organisers without a murmur.

The crew sailed fantastically together, not least because we managed to keep sailors of Vinny Lauwer's stature on board. Riding with us was not an easy decision for Vinny, in part because he had been having some trouble with his back. Several months after the 1994 Sydney to Hobart he began noticing that his lower spine was clicking about a lot. His doctors told him all was well but when I rang him to ask him if he would consider coming along on the '95 Hobart, his first reaction was: 'Yeah, okay, but I need to get my back checked out again because that clicking is getting worse and I am experiencing some pain.'

The doctors gave him the okay and he raced with us, impressing everyone on board with his strength, agility and seamanship. But after the race was over, he went back to the doctors once more. This time they sent him off for an X-ray. I got a phone call later and Vinny told me what they had found – a break in his lower spine around T12/L1. Vinny had done the entire 1995 Sydney to Hobart yacht race with a broken back. We were not even aware that he was in pain, but I do not remember being surprised. He is that kind of guy.

What was happening was that the bones in Vinny's body were starting to degenerate, a condition apparently so rare that his physicians did not even think to check for it at first. Undeterred, Vinny went through several major operations, lasting sixteen and a half hours in total, to remove all the steel in his back from the first break and replace it with more steel and bone grafts. He kept searching for sponsors and funding so that he could finish building the boat that would take him around the world. No one who knew him had any doubt he would finally do it.

SWD, too, was forging ahead, the *Carpe Diem* finishing every major race it entered, which is no mean feat in itself. When we finally did have to pull out of an event – the 1996 Sydney to Hobart, because of a broken boom just near Eden on the southern New South Wales coast – the shock was incredible. The crew had never faced such a disappointment before. Not only was the boat finishing every race, it was finishing well, and the realisation that the boom was damaged so badly that we were going to have to pull out left the race crew shellshocked.

'How can we fix it?' came the cry as we desperately tried to think of a way around the crippled vessel's injury. 'What can we do?'

Nothing, was the answer. Nothing.

We pressed on. Within the organisation, we worked out our priorities. SWD was about creating opportunities for the disabled to be seen to be competing against the best in the world in an even-handed way. Sailing is a skill-based sport, and ocean racing is very demanding – technically, mentally and physically. We needed more able-bodied people on board – a hard decision with several reasons underpinning it.

The first was that we could not exclude ourselves from the rest of society. Having made our point in 1994, creating a 100 per cent disabled crew was slightly going against what Sailors with disAbilities was aiming for. Our main aim was to prove that disabled people could achieve things on the same terms as the able-bodied. Life is integrated, so the sailing had to be as well. Up to a point, of course. There should always be more disabled than able-bodied sailors on board. To achieve our aims, and to get ourselves noticed, we had to become truly competitive. If we took the *Carpe Diem* out in a major yacht race and floated around the ocean at the back of the pack, everyone would just pat us on the head, something disabled people are very used to. I was sick of it.

If we were going be in a race, we had to be in it up to our armpits. This meant that the *Carpe Diem* had to change. The boat that I raced in the Sydney to Hobart in 1994 was the boat I had built to go cruising around the world in with my wife. It was a comfortable, benign, beautifully-rigged 54-footer with cedar panelling. Well, the panelling could stay, but Sailors with disAbilities needed a lean, mean racing machine and as the years ticked by that is what the *Carpe Diem* became.

We replaced the mast, put a bigger rudder in, and changed the keel – a terrifying proposition for me because it meant putting my precious boat in dry dock and cutting a huge hole in the bottom 10 feet long and two feet wide. We changed the sails, bought more tailor-made spinnakers and fitted a lifting keel on the boat, turning it from a cruiser to a racer–cruiser. Every change made it faster, and cost more money. Aspect Computing became our premier sponsor, thanks to CEO Pete Draney, who started joking that supporting us meant he was going to go to heaven.

By 1997 we were becoming a force to be reckoned with. The *Carpe Diem* was competing in virtually every single east-coast race and doing more sea miles than almost any other boat we knew.

The documentary made during the 1994 Hobart campaign began running on cable television, which meant it appeared year after year after year. Every time it screened, we would get calls from disabled people who had seen it and wanted to know more. As many as could make it ended up on the boat, and some even became part of our racing crew.

Not everybody had the right temperament for it. Yacht races – particularly the big ones – require a particular kind of stamina. Being race-fit means being able to cope with three days or more of almost total deprivation – little sleep and probably not much food – underpinned by a sheer determination to get to the finishing line. Crews are selected from people who can handle that. About 60 per cent of them would be disabled and about 40 per cent able-bodied. Many we would have to train up, which tested my patience to the limit and as many people will tell you, I am not a patient man.

Al Grundy threatened to leave the organisation completely after the 1994 Hobart because of the way I kept flying off the handle. People who came in perfectly ready to learn and become part of the team stormed off when I shouted at them. Part of the problem is that when I see something that is blatantly obvious to me, and nobody else sees it, I think to myself, I'm the dyslexic, I'm the fuckwit, I am the guy that can't pass exams, I am the dumb one in this outfit. And yet I can see that rope needs rolling up and putting away before someone catches themselves on it and trips off the side of the boat. All of you guys have spent the last twenty minutes walking over the top of it. What the hell are you playing at?

It takes me back to that first day with my therapist, Val, and my distorted point of reference. The problem is not that somebody else has made a mistake, it is that I always think I am the dill. When someone else – i.e. someone who can read – makes a mistake, part of me thinks they must be doing it on purpose and I fly off the handle. On a boat, as skipper, the rule is always safety first. You cannot mess around with people's safety. But there are ways and ways of saying things.

One fine day Cathy Josling, a friend of Sharon Bond, who had in turn become a firm friend to me, made me have a really big think about my behaviour. We had a guy on board who was a Pommy traveller. He was a well-meaning able-bodied bloke who was very keen to help out; a young professional, which meant he was probably very bright, but he simply could not get the hang of sailing. He sailed with us a few times, and then walked off the boat one day in disgust because I started laying into him.

Cathy told me through gritted teeth that I had to stop treating people like that. It was not the first time she'd taken me to task for letting my temper get the better of me, and she does not even remember this occasion today. I do, though, because it was the first time I really listened.

Her message was clear. I would just keep losing people because of the way I was treating them. I was constantly attacking them and they were taking it personally. There were other ways of doing things.

That stopped me in my tracks. I was not pleased to hear it but I couldn't stop thinking about it. She was right. So I started trying to be a little bit more diplomatic, with varying degrees of success. A big incentive was what was happening with the kids' days.

Albert Lee was one of those who kicked off the kids' days – or Youth Program, as we later officially called it – back in 1994, during the run-up to the Sydney to

Hobart. These were outings where we took disadvantaged and disabled children out on the boat. No sooner had it started than everyone realised what great fun they were and how much everybody – kids and adults alike – got out of them. By 1996 we were running them seriously. The more we did it, the more schools heard about it. They started ringing us. We took the program down the coast a few years later.

Doing it depended on having a crew willing to help out, so it became a condition of sailing that you had to put your hours in with the kids' days. No one was paid – no one ever has been in the history of SWD – but a lot of our sailors absolutely leapt on them. Every day was different. We would have Down's syndrome children, those who had cancer, those with different congenital physical and mental problems, and those who were recovering from accidents.

Some of the kids would be terrified to get on the boat but as soon as their carers coaxed them up, the pleasure they would get from it was phenomenal. We started learning pretty quickly what kinds of kids could cope with what. Putting the mainsail up can be noisy, which freaked some of them out, so we learned to warn them. If it got too blowy out in Sydney Harbour, we would drop the sails and motor along. Every now and again it would be too rough to ride out, so we would rig up the bosun's chair and take them up the mast, one by one, for a ride.

We started doing kids' days on the trips back to Sydney from Queensland after the races of the Northern

Campaign. On one such run, we had been away for six weeks and were exhausted. We were finding showers and dry towels anywhere we could, and wearing underpants so dirty you had to nail them down the night before so that they would still be there when you woke up the following morning. I had come to love working with children but I sorely needed a break.

The sessions continued relentlessly, and one morning, in a mixed group of ten or so children, I was introduced to a boy called David. He was fourteen with quite long limbs, but he had cerebral palsy and so little muscle that he needed not only a wheelchair but also supports for his head and neck because he couldn't hold them up.

I took one look at him and thought, this is going to be difficult. Getting him on board, keeping him on board, even taking him out of his wheelchair appeared problematic. I was seriously wondering if this would be the first time we'd have to turn someone down when his sister collared me and told me how long he had been looking forward to this trip and how very much he wanted to do it. As she spoke, David watched me with his big, bright eyes, looking so fragile that he was about to fall in half. He was unable, it seemed, to move or say a word.

We went downstairs, pulled bedding off the bunks and built up a place for him in the cockpit with cushions and pillows. The thing we should have had, and that we have now, is a beanbag – perfect for squishing kids into. But we were still learning back then. So we created this big comfortable shape in the cockpit, picked David up and put him in it facing backwards, for safety's sake.

As we sailed out into the ocean, the other kids were roaming around the boat and having a great time whooping and cheering as the SWD team looked after them. David's sister came up to me and told me that he wanted to go up to the front of the boat, too. Oh no, I thought, but got two of the guys to pick him up and carefully take him there. Then the other children started mucking around in the middle of the boat, so of course David wanted to be there as well.

By this stage, the best way to support David seemed to be with another human body, so I had him cradled in my arms. As we headed back inland after several hours of sailing, we let the kids take turns steering the boat, and when they were done and we were on our way back to the harbour, I got behind the wheel with David. He had some movement in a couple of the fingers on his left hand, and could reach out, so I put his left hand on the steering wheel and he helped me dock the boat. Safely in, we all got off and started saying our goodbyes to the kids. David was back in his wheelchair and I went up to him, tapped him on the shoulder and said: 'Thanks for coming out today, mate. I know that was difficult and I thought you did a great job.'

As I went to walk away, I felt something stop me. David had hooked his left hand under my sleeve and was tugging me down to his level. His wheelchair had a screen, and by moving his right knee up and down he was able to operate a device that threw the words onto his screen and even allowed his computer to speak audibly. He kept pumping his knee up and down until he got to the phrase 'Thank

you, I've had a wonderful day', and he made his comput-
erised voice repeat it over and over again, while he held me
so closely to him I could feel his shallow breath. All of a
sudden the dirty underpants and wet towels really didn't
matter any more. Everything fell back into perspective.

So the kids' days continued, between the training and
the racing, and then, one day, a group of dyslexic
children came on board for a ride, and Travis Foley
appeared. Travis was eleven and a tiny little bugger for
his age, so small I kept thinking you could put him in a
matchbox. At first he seemed just like all the other kids
in a freckle-faced, redheaded sort of way. He had long,
fine fingers, a big, mischievous toothy grin and no shoulders to speak of. There was no reason, really, to look at
him twice. Until he started asking questions. He had
never been on a boat before and he couldn't get over how
big it was. He wanted to know every little thing about
it – the length, the breadth, which rope did what, why
the sails were where they are, how the steering worked,
where the Mars Bars were kept. He was bright, sharp
and shining with curiosity.

'This is so much fun,' he beamed at me. 'It's brilliant.
Just brilliant.'

'Travis,' I said as he skipped his way off the boat, 'do
you want to come back?'

'Yes, yes, yes,' he hissed.

I got someone to grab his mother Cherie's phone
number in country NSW, where they lived, and asked her
if she minded Travis doing some real training with us.
Cherie came up to meet us and agreed, partly, as she

later told me, because being on board was having a huge effect on the boy.

Meeting Travis was a real revelation to me. I had had children with dyslexia on board before, but this was the first time I had become close to one of them, particularly one whose situation so mirrored my own. Travis's problems had emerged early in his life. He too had a younger sister, Natasha, who leapt upon reading from an early age. He was going through school and learning virtually nothing, and the other kids were teasing him, much as they had teased me. He would leave the playground with chants of 'Clever Trevor' ringing in his ears. Cherie, a single mum, was doing her best to push his self-esteem back up where it should have been and keep the rest of her family together, but poor young Travis was becoming very withdrawn, 'retreating', as his mother put it, 'right into his shell'.

What really surprised me, though, was the casual cruelty and humiliation that he was being put through at school. Years later Cherie would discover that one of Travis's teachers had stood him up in front of his classmates and told him to read out loud. Now, Travis's level of dyslexia is about the same as mine – he can barely even spell his own name – and a teacher who knew he could not read was humiliating him in front of his classmates. What kind of a sadist does that? Had things really changed so little since I was a child?

On board the boat you would never have known there was a problem. Travis immediately started taking the boat apart in his mind and working out how everything on board operated and what needed to be done. His openness and curiosity impressed me. Back on dry land, it was clear that he had never met an adult with dyslexia as bad as his. He kept asking me who really owned the *Carpe Diem*.

'I do,' I told him.

'Uh-huh,' he would say, sliding his eyes away from my face back down to the ground in what looked like disappointment. I knew I would be hearing the question again.

One day after a training sail, he waited until everyone else had wandered off. 'Okay,' he said, looking over his shoulder to check that we really were alone. 'Now you can tell me. Who really owns this boat?'

I told him what I always told him. 'I own the boat, Travis. I really do.'

'Right,' he said. 'I get it. You're not really dyslexic, are you?'

As the kids' days progressed, becoming absolutely integral to Sailors with disAbilities, I had started thinking about taking a child on a major ocean yacht race. There were no rules against it and, while it would be risky, I felt it was something we could and probably should do. The more I watched Travis, the more I wondered, is this the kid?

We started selecting the 1998 Sydney to Hobart crew. Al Grundy, who had done every Sydney to Hobart up until then, decided to take the Christmas shift at Bioscientific, so his workmates wouldn't have to.

I phoned Travis's mother. 'Cherie,' I said, 'it's Dave.

I've been thinking. We'd love Travis to do the Sydney to Southport race with us this year. And after that, we would like him to come on board and do the Sydney to Hobart. He will probably be the youngest sailor in the fleet.'

Silence.

'It's a big race, but I think he will manage it. We'll look after him.'

'I don't know . . .' she began.

'Look, I understand why you would be worried. The Sydney to Hobart is a big race, and it can be a dangerous one. But I promise you, Cherie, I will bring him back. If Travis doesn't come home from this, I don't come home either.'

As I put the phone down my words kept ringing in my ears.

11

DECEMBER 26, 1998: I flipped open *The Australian* and my heart sank into my deck shoes. Today was a beautifully sunny summer day, but the lines running across the isobaric chart forecast on the weather page – the only page of any newspaper that is of any use to me – showed what looked like a vacuum sitting on Bass Strait. Oh Jesus, I thought to myself. Nature does not like a vacuum.

I raced down to Rushcutters Bay and did my best to cut through the manic pre-race hustle and bustle at the CYC and find Clouds – our weather forecaster Roger Badham – who had been up much of the night assessing computer models of the upcoming weather patterns for the *Aspect Computing* (as our boat was known for this race), and a chain of other boats.

'What's the gig, mate?' I asked him. 'What are we in for?'

'You are going to get kicked today,' Clouds replied severely, handing me a briefcase with his full analysis in it. 'There is going to be a lot of wind.'

'How much?'

Clouds shrugged. 'A lot.'

'For how long?'

'Twenty-four hours, I'd say.'

I rubbed my beard and looked at him.

Okay, I thought. Okay. If it is going to be over in twenty-four hours, I can deal with that.

Outside the Cruising Yacht Club the scene was manic. The crowd of spectators – everyone from would-be sailors looking for last-minute rides to high-heeled, exquisitely dressed socialites – was swelling by the minute. Crew members had to push their way through a confusion of handshakes, backslaps and cheering throngs just to find their boats.

Some found it harder than others. Paul Borg had come down from Mooloolaba in Queensland to work as mastman on the *Aspect*. He had lost his sight as a result of a progressive eye disease and was navigating the wooden walkways with the help of a white cane – an easy mark for the television and newspaper bloodhounds sniffing around for colour before the race began.

Danny Kane, our 'kicker', who looked after the rope that controls the spinnaker, was another obvious target for the waiting journalists, his withered, white-slinged left arm and stumbling gait testament to a stroke that felled him after he underwent surgery to fix a shoulder he had dislocated snowboarding. Danny, whose paralysed

211

left arm and leg were slowly regaining some of their former movement, had been with SWD for eighteen months, during which time he had visibly come out of his shell and become more than a little used to having microphones stuck under his nose every time he got on or off the *Aspect*. He, like everyone else, was only carrying a very small bag with the bare essentials he would need for the race. Every extra ounce on board would slow the boat down and we were here to race, so the crew were pared down to their basics, most of them having already stowed their racing essentials – wet weather gear, thermals, polar fleece and tracksuit pants – on board the *Aspect* a few days earlier. Anything else they thought they were going to need at the other end was already on its way by plane to Hobart.

By 9.30 am the dizzying smell of bacon sizzling on the CYC's barbecue was wafting across *Aspect*'s deck and the crew members were making their way on board, one by one. My second in command, Kim Jaggar, appeared looking cool and relaxed as ever. Kim, the principal of Sydney Boys High School, had lost his left arm in a skiing accident and was a very tough, reliable and considered character.

Harald Mirlieb, deaf as a post and the best bowman I knew, was leaning against the mast looking remarkably relaxed. Young Travis was dressed immaculately in the crew uniform of pressed blue shirt and black Aspect cap, but was almost shaking with nerves as he left his mother and sister Natasha and climbed on board.

The mix was roughly 50 per cent disabled, 50 per cent

able-bodied, but of the disabled sailors, three – Harald, myself and Kim Jaggar – were experienced Hobart veterans. Some of the ABs, such as mastman Glenn 'Jack' Frost, navigator Cathy Josling and sail trimmer Sharon Bond, had done miles of sea and were also proven hands. For others it was their first ever Hobart and the stress was showing.

Sandy Collins, a fit, feisty, level-headed school administrator in her fifties, had been sailing for several years but had never attempted a Sydney to Hobart before, and was so churned up she had already locked her keys inside her car.

The 'twenty-four hours' prediction weighed heavily on my mind. I had another look at *The Australian* and trotted off to the Bureau of Meteorology's stand at the CYC to rub shoulders with the other concerned skippers. A low was forming and we did not know how bad it was. I talked things over with Kim and decided, yes, let's get into the ocean and into this race. By the time we were halfway down the New South Wales coast we would have a better idea of what we were dealing with. There were plenty of places along that stretch of coast to run to if we needed.

I thought the five of us who had done the race before could pull the others through it. If the rest of the team were downstairs, Kim and I could be steering, the other three rotating around, coming on deck when we needed them.

Climbing back on board at about ten-thirty, I started our normal race procedure with my traditional 'Okay, guys, settle down' speech. There were procedures we needed to run through and safety drills we had to double-check – making sure everybody had their harness, one last check that the life-rafts were where they should be and A-OK. The food needed checking, and the gas and water, and the engine, all as slowly as possible to calm things down.

At about eleven o'clock we started to have a bit of a talk about what we were expecting from the weather and what that was going to mean for days one, two and three of the race. A few cups of coffee appeared. I don't really like the crew to eat immediately before the start in case they get seasick. I turned to face them on the deck. 'What we know is that there is a howling, pretty stiff nor'easter outside, south of the Heads. It will probably be a fast spinnaker ride all afternoon and into the night – I am expecting a very fast race for the first twelve to fourteen hours.

'Beyond that, things are a little uncertain. This could be a rough one, guys. The weather report is forecasting a lot of wind and there may be some action over Bass Strait. A few of you will not have seen conditions like this before.

'There is a bad twenty-four hours ahead but it looks like it's only going to be twenty-four hours. We can deal with that. We're good sailors, and we can use the rough patch to our advantage.'

Sobered but excited, the crew started to prepare the boat, getting the mainsail up and picking which head-sails we thought we were going to use, laying them out in the right order on the floor. Soon there were sails everywhere downstairs. The key was having those we thought we would need up on the top of the pile for easy access.

We threw off the moorings and made our way into the crowded bedlam that was Sydney Harbour. We had a TV commitment, a boat-to-boat interview between a journalist and Travis, who was now twelve years old and by far the youngest competitor in the race. Unfortunately for the TV crew, Travis was so overwhelmed that he stood at the back of the boat like a terrified wooden cigar store Indian with his arms around one of the struts that carried our solar panels (to generate electricity for the boat), answering their questions with a simple 'Yes', 'No', 'Yes', 'No'.

As one o'clock loomed, we picked our way towards the start line, dodging thousands of every kind of spectator craft imaginable to get to the gun. The voices of everybody from Al Grundy to Cherie Foley rang out over the water from nearby vessels, singing out 'Good luck', 'Godspeed' and 'Kick butt'. The crew stayed focused, barely daring to acknowledge them.

The start of the Hobart is always the same, very pumpy, full of adrenalin-fuelled men having a go at each other, and I suppose I do more than my share of that, so that last half-hour before the one o'clock deadline disappears in your mind, sliding down like a telescope, crowding down into itself until – bang! – there's the ten-minute gun, and those ten minutes turn into ten seconds.

Olympic swimming star Susie O'Neill pulled a ceremonial cord and the starter's cannon roared, leaving a puff of acrid smoke hanging over Sydney Harbour. It was 1300 hours – what the *Aspect* and the other 114 boats pulsing to get into the fray had been waiting for. Someone was screaming port, someone else was screaming starboard and the next thing you know there are two boats on top of you, and for the next thirty seconds all you can see is a collage of sails and water, with voices yelling over the din. You somehow find separation and start to move up through the Harbour, trying to find your way across the fleet and get out of everyone else's wind.

We escaped from the early fray unscathed. *Nokia*, an 83-footer and the biggest vessel in the race, had already hit *Bright Morning Star* and *Sword of Orion*, leaving scars of varying damage on all three. Red flags flew up – there would be an inquiry but it would have to wait. No time now to sort out whose fault it was as the pack began powering its way towards the first buoy off South Head.

Sayonara, carrying the closely-cropped media mogul Lachlan Murdoch, who had been waved off by his fiancée Sarah O'Hare, charged ahead of the fleet. We picked our way through the competition with what was left of the wind, running very, very slowly. *Aspect* got pinned down on the left-hand side and I could not get her back over to the right, where we wanted to be. I started tacking and we finally struggled through the Heads – we must have been two-thirds of the way down the fleet by the time we got out into the ocean, which is not a good look for a 54-footer.

Finally, the seaward mark. All we could see were boats ahead of us. The big yellow kite filled and the *Aspect* spread her wings, charging down the New South Wales coast with a nor'easter of between 15 and 25 knots behind us. All afternoon we burned past boat after boat after boat with about 18 knots of wind and 4 knots of current running south, making our travel speed around 22 knots: a magic ride. We made Point Perpendicular and Jervis Bay in five hours flat, about the same time it would take in a motor car. The fleet's pace was so fast that back on dry land, some were speculating that this might be the year the Sydney to Hobart race record was broken.

On board the *Aspect* the atmosphere was electric. 'This is going to be a good one,' said Sandy as the wind tore through her blonde hair. 'This is going to be great.'

It stayed great. That afternoon, only one other boat passed us, *Spirit of Downunder*. By the time the sun dipped beneath the horizon we had caught up with most of the boats and were right on the tail of the front-runners. The huge maxi *Nokia*, with its complement of twenty-six crew members – twice as many as most of the other yachts carried – was hammering down the coast with a mate of mine on board. He later told me that one of the other crew members came up on deck and told him, 'Hey, we're smoking.'

'You see that yellow spinnaker over there?' he replied, pointing us out in the dwindling twilight. '*Nokia* is 80 foot, that's *Aspect* and it's 50 foot and right on our tail. So watch it – that little 50-footer is going to get us if we're not careful.'

We picked up a weather report which showed that the low over Bass Strait was deepening severely. That was bad news. The deeper the low, the more intense and powerful the wind: the two run parallel to each other. I looked down from mid-deck and thought, hmm, remembering that Clouds had said, 'Twenty-four hours.' The boat was really tough, and I had no worries about it. The thing to do was keep flying.

Day turned to night as we soared further south down the New South Wales coast, the darkness highlighting a magnificent electrical storm ahead. Magnificent but terrifying. As the *Aspect* charged ahead, the storm moved either side of us. Enormous lightning bolts probably 20 miles away from us were crashing into the sea on one side, and the land on the other.

'Where are we going to go?' called out one of the guys. The storm was limiting our options. Dead ahead it was still clear: there was a hole running through the storm there. We headed straight into it.

The wind freshened to about 30 knots, and we changed the spinnaker down to our 1.5-ounce hound spinnaker. The wind was blowing north and north-west, shaking the boat so violently that anything larger might have torn the rig from the deck. Under the smaller sail, the *Aspect* settled down a bit.

We were getting pushed out to sea by the wind and were heading further east and south than the race demanded but I was not unhappy with that. We could lay a line through the Tasman to Hobart fairly easily from anywhere along here, and my main concern was that we should be as far away from the continental shelf as we could, because if we were going to hit a really big sea I did not want to be in shallow water when the waves might be at their highest. I wanted the boat to be in the deeps.

Out of our sight and radio reach, some boats were already dropping out of the race and heading into land with damage. The *Aspect* was sailing well, clipping along at about 22 knots, whooping, hollering and charging forward as she launched off waves and crashed into the troughs beyond. But the sea was getting bigger and the wind was closing in. The only way I could see through the storm was the archway between the lightning clouds on either side of us, so we kept trying to sail the *Aspect* through it. Without warning, our narrow corridor closed off completely.

Lightning tore into the water all around us. We were in the middle of the ocean in the heart of an electrical storm, and the best lightning conductor in the world is an aluminium stick pointing right up into the sky. This was very dangerous indeed. Bolts of lightning crashed down from above us and thumped into the sea, each strike beginning with a deafening crack, lighting up the whole sea in a hideous, split-second, 360 degree parody of daylight. The lightning branded the outlines of other boats on the horizon – they disappeared just as quickly back into the bleak night. We were not talking to them – you shut down inter-vessel communication during a race. Just as well – we needed to concentrate on what was happening to us. Around the boat the sea was starting to churn more roughly. Young Travis was already getting seasick below.

As the gusts and waves increased we had a couple of roundups with the spinnaker. A roundup happens when you are running with the wind behind you and the boat goes out of control. It may be that the steerer – in this case me – makes a mistake and the bow of the boat comes out a little bit too far. The wind comes into the back of the boat and spins it back around into the direction of the wind. When you are doing 20 knots and you round up, it is like being in a washing machine. Everything tumbles, spins, gets thrown around everywhere on the bow. The people above deck are tossed all over each other, and they have to desperately hang onto anything they can so that they don't get washed off. Even with a safety harness tethering you to the side, you do not want to be clinging on overboard in those conditions.

I was pushing the boat hard because I wanted to get as far south as I could. Every mile we covered now was going to make our lives that much easier when the blow that I knew was coming finally reached us. A mile achieved now would be like 10 miles in the blow. We had to struggle on.

Without warning, the spinnaker declipped itself and fell into the ocean. We were bare-poled and drifting in the middle of a storm, out of control. With panting ferocity, the above-deck crew dragged it back up on board.

'We've got to get the boat ready for what's coming,' I shouted through the howling wind. 'Get the storm gear up to steerage and find the big turnbuckle. We need it.'

It was pitch-black, about 2 am, and Sandy Collins was on watch. She later told me that when she heard those words, her heart sank. We had done our emergency training offshore that summer, and on one of those training runs I had ordered the big turnbuckle – a two-foot-long metal attachment to the inner forestay that tightens the rig up really tight; you clip the sail onto it and hoist the storm-stay sail up – be attached to the foredeck. She was working on the foredeck at that time and jumped below deck to find it. Poking her head back up with the turnbuckle in her hand, she said, 'David, at what point do we use this?'

I replied, 'When you don't want to play any more. When all you want to do is say "Beam me up, Scotty". When you say aaaaarrrgh!'

As Sandy braced herself against the storm and felt the turnbuckle get passed into her hand, she thought, oh shit, things must be pretty bad.

Storm gear up, I started heading closer to our course line. Suddenly the wind died down completely. I spun my head around, trying to see what was coming. It was much too quiet. The tension on the boat became almost palpable. We were into the early hours of the morning and everybody knew something awful was about to hit. At 2.13 am a new race forecast came through.

> WIND: W/SW *winds 25/35 knots, with stronger gusts. Winds increasing to the south of Merimbula offshore, reaching 40/50 knots this afternoon as low deepens.*

> WAVES: *2 to 3 metres, rising to 4 to 5 metres offshore in the south.*
> SWELL: *1 to 2 metres, rising to 3 to 4 metres offshore south of Merimbula.*

The storm had been upgraded. A monster was on its way.

We waited and waited, shortening the sails to keep the boat moving, pushing south as fast as we could, always pushing south. Every one of us started wondering how good we really were. How were we going to cope with what lay ahead?.

Things quietened further. The lightning started to abate. Then 'Mayday, mayday' pierced the air from the radio station down below. *Challenge Again* had a man overboard. We checked our relative positions. There was nothing we could do.

I went off watch at 3 am, handed the helm over to Kim Jaggar, crawled into one of the narrow bunks and shut my eyes. Having made the mistake before of refusing to sleep on a major ocean race, I was not about to jeopardise the safety of the crew by doing the same thing now.

Outside, 4 am ticked past. The rain began falling, softly at first, then driving hard into the soft bodies above deck, confining visibility even further. When the rain sets in on an ocean yacht, especially at night, the world becomes very small. You can not see past it – all you deal with is your boat, by touch when you have to. It's a freezing, slithery world that extends only as far as the length of your arm.

Beyond the boat, the wind conditions were changing. First it came out of the west. Then it went south. Then back to the west, shooting up to 30 knots. Then it stopped. The boat was ready. The *Aspect* had her storm-stay sails up, her mainsail down completely and a crew waiting for what it knew was coming.

All at once the weather was upon us. Quietly at first, with the smell of gumleaves and dirt. The tempo quickened, the wind going from 10 knots to 40 knots in a matter of seconds. The boat was barely moving, so it lurched violently to port like a boxer receiving a king hit. It staggered, as though gathering breath, and charged into the fray. There was yelling, the noise of winches tightening and the wind screaming. Racing a boat is about changing gears and changing gears fast, and the months of training were beginning to pay off.

Forty knots of wind turned into 50 knots, 55 knots, 60 knots – harder and harder, higher and higher. The nightmare was under way. Danny Kane, hanging on for grim death up on the rail, could not believe what he was seeing. It was his first big race and he yelled out to one of the guys sitting beside him: 'Is it always like this?'

'No,' came the reply. 'This is rough.'

At 6 am I rolled out of my bunk and headed back up top for the next watch. As I clambered above deck on the tilting boat, the transparent dodger built into the companionway protected my face from the wind. I scanned the seascape. It was light but grey, really grey. Someone had taken away the sun. No other boats were visible – the vessels that were still in the race had scattered in every direction in preparation for what was to come – but the white-flecked sea was getting very, very big. Spume was coming off the tops of the waves, which meant it was starting to get rough. When a wave rolls and curls white, a big wind picks that white foam off and throws it across the top of the wave. Horizontal. That was just starting to happen, and the waves themselves were turning into towering mountains, getting closer together and moving straight up and straight down. Vertical.

The thing that sailors do is feel the breeze on their face, through their hair, on their cheeks. Inside the dodger I was protected from that. It wasn't until I stepped out that I copped it. The full force of the wind was quite literally staggering.

The boat was sliding away from the coastline into Bass Strait. We were three to four hours into the storm and it was pretty clear there would be another twenty hours to come. The boat was well out to sea off Gabo Island and 30 miles south. Decision time: do we turn around and head for home, or engage Bass Strait?

I got behind the wheel, taking over from Kim. We talked it over. If we turned towards Eden on the New South Wales coast, could we get to land from here, through these conditions? If we were going to try it, now was the time.

I called it. 'I think what we'll do is go for another three hours, until after my watch, and at 9 am we'll have a think about what comes next,' I said. 'Because right now we have no reason to go back. The boat is strong enough, the crew is performing, they are doing the things they are supposed to have done, and I'm happy. As far as I am concerned, everything is going alright.'

Kim agreed, and ducked below for a rest. Downstairs, it was pandemonium. The interior of the boat, which always took in some water through the rudder post at the back, was awash. The seals were not as good as they should have been. Everything – the beds, the sails, every bag in the boat – was soaked through and sea water was sloshing around inside the *Aspect* like surf. What I couldn't see was that the offwatch team had started bailing to keep the conditions below deck under some kind of control. They would stand at the bottom of the stairs, bail, bail, bail, and dump the water into the sink where it could drain back into the churning grey ocean. It was a difficult, claustrophobic job that had even the likes of Sandy and Sharon, who rarely got seasick, turning very green. Each person would do it for as long as they could, then come above deck briefly to recover.

Exhausted, the off-watchers would then dive into a bunk under a cold, sodden sleeping bag and almost pass out as the boat crashed, crashed and crashed again over the ever-swelling waves. Danny Kane, always slow to take his wet weather gear off because of his useless arm, was not even bothering to undress. He just lay down on whatever soaking sail was out of everyone else's way, and closed his eyes, trying desperately to sleep.

Up in the cockpit the wind was so severe that all we could do was sit there, trying to keep control of the boat. The storm staysail locks kept blowing out of their tracks and the crew had to scrabble across and re-attach them, over and over again, getting washed down the length of the deck every time.

The waves grew, crashing over the *Aspect* so hard it was like being dumped in the surf. As the water flew across the deck I held my breath and waited until it let me back up for air, by which time I had been swept off my feet and left dangling by my harness like a tea bag, with no idea which way up I was. As the boat came over a wave, all that remained visible in the dark grey trough below was wild, menacing water. The spray coming off it was horizontal and hard, like forks slamming into my face. We were soaked through but I was not cold. That was one of the strange things about that year; the current was warm. The best thing I had taken with me was an old pair of ski goggles. With them over my eyes I could almost see in front of me; hood pulled down, visor pulled up, looking through a quarter-inch gap into the searing rain.

Coming off watch I dived into my bunk, closed my eyes and suddenly it was noon – time to prise my heavy lids open, have a quick look at our position and crawl back along the lurching boat to the helm. Geez, I thought, realising we were still within range of land. There was no reason to come off course. The boat was still strong, and she was humming. There was a truck-load of water coming through the rudder, but we could deal with that.

The next three hours were just belt, belt, belt, over the crest of each wave, continually trying to minimise the impact on the boat so it did not shake apart and leave us bobbing in the ocean. I could not afford to make a mistake because it would hurt us, badly. Steering, you can't think about the wave that just went through, you have to focus on the one you are dealing with, and what it might be telling you about the wave that is coming just behind it, because each wave can give you a clue as to what the next one will be all about.

As the waves built to 15 metres – higher than the height of our mast, the *Aspect* climbed to the top and was looking at a 30-metre drop into the trough of the next one. What I was desperately trying to avoid is something called 'dropping off', where the boat rushes up to the crest of the wave and instead of sliding down the other side, it launches itself out into space. The boat goes airborne and you hang onto whatever is at hand for the one . . . two . . . three . . . four sickening seconds of freefall. Then – bang! It crashes into the base of the wave with a deafening thud. The *Aspect* was built so that she could be lifted eight metres into the air and dropped onto solid concrete all day, every day. That's how strong she was. In those seas she needed every ounce of that strength, and more.

When the wave comes towards the boat, the helmsman has to turn it up into the wave, slowing it down as much as possible. Then, as the bow sticks across the crest of the wave, the helmsman pulls the boat around, dropping it a little over the far side of the crest so it slides crossways down the back of the wave and into the trough. But you can't stay in the trough because the waves are breaking, so you have to present your bow to take the break there. Up, over and down. Up, over and down. Again. And again. And again. If the helmsman gets it wrong, God help you. Come off the wave's crest too early, and a boat which was doing seven knots is suddenly doing 10 knots, screaming down the back of a huge mountain of water much faster than it should and slamming into the wave ahead. The next thing you know, you are airborne, and a boat that goes airborne may drop so far and fast it smashes into pieces in the trough below.

I was trying all sorts of techniques to slow the boat down and as the waves got bigger and my shift went on, we got through most of them pretty well, only dropping off one or two. But after three hours of this, at the end of your shift, mistakes creep up on you. It may be daylight but you can't see. The wind is driving rain horizontally into your face and it is hard work protecting your eyes all the time.

You set yourself up ready for the next wave and you feel the boat make the crest. You pull the boat up and have a little breather so you can slow it down as it races over the back of the wave. Then you turn your face away from the spume and the wind and grab a breath of air. You feel the boat settle and the next wave looms. All the while you're thinking, right, concentrate. Here we go again. Your arms are aching, your shoulders are on fire and all you want to do is get out from behind that wheel. I have done Sydney to Hobarts before and not slept because I felt I was needed on deck. With Kim on board, I was happy to go to sleep – not least because I was going to be needed in three hours and I had to get some rest.

Downstairs, though, the radio was heralding maydays that would come from all points of the compass. *Young Endeavour* was trying to get a fishing boat to *Team Jaguar*, mastless and drifting, hamstrung with a rope-tangled, useless propeller.

'Stay on radio watch,' I told Cathy. We didn't know where they were. They should have had two GPSs on board so I was dumbfounded as to why they couldn't find their position.

Another mayday: *Winston Churchill* is sinking and the crew have taken to life-rafts. Another yacht has been rolled. There is a problem on *Sword of Orion*. Peter, the skipper of *Kingurra*, has lost a man overboard. Poor bugger, I thought, he's gone. I was wrong – they managed to haul him back on board, but we did not find that out until long afterwards.

'Let people know where we are,' I told Cathy. 'If someone is close to us, say within a 10 mile radius, and in trouble, let me know and we'll talk about it. Until that happens we have got a lot on ourselves. Let's just deal with that.'

To turn around and go to the assistance of another boat in those conditions would have been a very difficult manoeuvre, and potentially a very dangerous one – a huge ask. Manoeuvring into position in winds of up to 70 knots, then trying to find the wounded vessel through 40 foot walls of water, was neither easy nor safe. One boat did. I saw it later on video and thought it was the bravest thing I had ever witnessed. Those guys deserved a medal.

On board the *Aspect* we had 10 tonnes of fibreglass launching itself into mid-air every 10 seconds. Not to mention the bilge water. We stood a 24-hour radio watch. Perhaps we would be needed. Someone – I have no idea who – shoved a cup of hot soup into my hand. I climbed into the bunk I shared with Kim, registering at the back of my mind that it was as wet inside the boat as it was outside, grabbed a sodden pillow, shoved it under my head and was out like a light.

We were dealing with some big, big waves and we could have done with another helmsman, but no one else on board was qualified to handle those conditions, so when I came off watch, Kim went back, grabbing the wheel with his one and only arm. He was tough, alright – I was finding the conditions tough enough with two arms. I could not begin to imagine how he was coping with just one.

Below deck, with me, the rest of the offwatch crew were coping as best they could. Danny Kane was crawling around on his backside, as his paralysed leg and arm meant he always had to when conditions got a little rough. He later said the big seas did not make too much difference to him. The only real change was that it put him on a par with the rest of the crew, because everyone else was having to crawl around as well.

Inside my soaking bunk, rigged to pin my prone body in close to the boat's wall so that I would not roll out every time the vessel lurched over on its side, I crashed immediately but not completely. The boat had a thumping rhythm as it went up and down the waves, but every now and again there would be silence – it had come off the back of a wave badly – and then a crash as the boat hit the water's surface with a sickening thud. Through the haze of semi-sleep I heard more reports coming in over the radio. Another boat in trouble, another flare, another mayday. People missing, vessels rolled. Experience told me what the reports did not: lives were being lost all around us. We were not close enough to anybody to be of any assistance. All we could do was try to get our own boat through it.

As the hours rolled on and the watches changed, we drove the boat through the churning ocean. We might not have been able to see them, but we could hear the big waves coming as the tops of them rolled, broke and crashed like trains coming towards the boat. Conditions got worse as the afternoon dragged on. By 3 pm we were getting washed around the cockpit, despite being strapped in with our safety harnesses, by blue – not white – water. The new watch dragged themselves up on a boat leaning at 45 degrees, clipped themselves on and pulled each other to the rail where they sat on the side of the boat watching out for other boats, for waves, for anything. When they spotted a big one coming through, they yelled out a warning to the helmsman and braced themselves to have the breath knocked out of them as they were slammed against the rail by massive waterfalls screaming over the deck and back into the ocean. Each crew member then grabbed his or her line, pulled bodies that were being knocked black and blue back into position and waited for the next one.

Every big wave that came through tore me off the steering wheel as well, so for the few seconds it took me to scramble back, the boat, with nobody at the helm, was out of control – a really dangerous situation. How Kim was managing with just one arm I will never know. He ended up almost breaking his ankle after getting hit by waves and washed across the cockpit, but he kept the boat on track.

The wind was so high that our deck instruments showing windspeed and boatspeed were no longer working. The last windspeed reading Danny Kane recalled seeing before they went under was 78 knots. It got worse than that – Wilson's Promontory in Bass Strait recorded a ferocious, cyclonic 92 knots that day.

Every now and again the storm board would slide back, Travis's head would come out, he would puke and the storm would wash the debris away within seconds. The others were all dealing with varying degrees of nausea.

Sail trimmer Suzy Oram and Sandy snuggled up to each other briefly at one stage, very scared indeed. Although she didn't tell anyone until afterwards, Sandy was convinced we were not going to make it. Her seventeen-year-old son Gareth had planned to race on one of the other boats but had dropped out when they had to replace its rig and he decided he was not interested in sailing on an untried rig. All she could think was that she was so glad he was not in the heart of the storm with the other competitors.

Suzy was about to start a new phase in her life. She had just got engaged and told Sandy she had left the ring at home because she did not want to lose it. Her fiancé was manning another boat but she had no idea they had already pulled out of the race at Eden.

Downstairs, the gas canister got loose and threatened to smash a gaping hole in the boat. Somebody grabbed it and lashed it down – a good decision safety-wise but it meant there was no chance of hot drinks, let alone any hot food. The boat was keeled over so far I do not think we could have got the stove going anyway. I went on watch with my pockets jampacked full of lollies, sitting there for three hours stuffing sugar into my mouth to keep the adrenalin and concentration going. Elsewhere, people were putting a brave face on things.

Cathy was in the navigator's station, which is downstairs on the starboard side, the high side of the boat, held fast in her seat with straps around her belly to stop her flying across the boat. She stayed there for fourteen hours at a trot, with the boat at an angle of 30 degrees so she was right over on her ear, doing the radio work and navigating. She would find massive bruising coming through when she unbuckled.

Everyone was doing their job, and supporting each other. There were nerves, yes, but nobody panicked. We tried to keep the worst of it from Travis, but the 24-hour radio watch meant there was no escape from the knowledge that boats were in trouble all around us. We could not see them but we knew that they were there.

Travis grabbed Cathy at one point. 'Are you scared?' she asked him.

'Yes, I am,' he replied. It was the first and last time he voiced his fear.

'It will be okay,' she told him. 'We are all going to be okay.'

She relayed his words to me and I thought, good, there is no bullshit going on. He is dealing with it.

Those upstairs huddled together in the cockpit, clipped on and hanging on, concentrating on the waves. No one talked much. There was some sickness, yes, but every crew member I saw was going really well. The boat's rig was standing up nice and straight, so it was a case of keep going, we'll get there. We would cope. We would have to.

At the 6 pm change of watch the new crew harnessed up. They automatically slung on their safety bumbags, each containing a strobe light, dye marker, a wine bladder (which, when blown up, would aid flotation), a knife and a fluoro cap, which I decided to make everyone buy after Harald jumped in for one of the man-overboard training sessions three miles out to sea wearing one, and we realised how much more visible they made any head floating in the ocean. The last and most useful piece of equipment in each bumbag was a personal EPIRB – Emergency Position Indicating Radio Beacon – designed to transmit distress signals and the precise location of their position via satellite.

As darkness fell we heard over the radio that one of the other vessels was having GPS problems and could not work out where it was in the huge seas. It was sending flares up in the hope that other boats could spot it.

We brought three or four extra people up on deck to keep a lookout but we did not see them.

Night-time, again. We were well into Bass Strait by then, in seriously deep seas. The wave pattern changed; they weren't as steep as they had been in the shallower water. The training and discipline took over as my mind seemed to separate from my aching body and the relentless change of shifts rolled on through the steely watches of the night.

That night and on through the early hours of the morning, it was simply a matter of keeping going, eyes scanning desperately for any sign of lights – however dim – on the horizon. A roar penetrates the pitch black; it suddenly sounds like you are trapped in an underground railway line with a train powering towards you. Another big wave is about to hit: 'Oh shit, not again.'

If you are lucky you have the bow at the right angle and the wave sweeps the boat in blue water, you get washed out from behind the stern, your feet end up above your head, your tether holds you down. It is a mass of ropes and water and confusion. The wave leaves the cockpit, and as it goes down you fall behind the steering wheel with a crash. You are back on deck, still in the dark. You turn yourself around and there is another wave coming at you so you have to get yourself back behind the steering wheel, straighten up as quickly as you can and hope the boat's okay.

Even when you are being turned upside-down, you are still trying to steer the boat as best you can, making sure the boat is where it should be. Every now and again the hatch slides open, a head comes out and drops a load of green bile on the cockpit. It's all over your legs, everything. Oh, that's disgusting, but every wave that comes through is swooshing it out, so who cares?

Down below, in the rank-smelling sauna that is now the inside of the boat, the radio watch continues, the bilge is being pumped, and the remains of the exhausted crew are sleeping as best they can in the tangle of ropes, sails and sodden bedding. By now the bunks are largely empty. The floor has become the safest place to sleep because you could not fall off it.

By 6 o'clock on that second morning we had a staysail up. I don't think I spoke to anyone coming off watch, except for Cathy, the navigator, to check our position and tracking. It was a bloody tough ride but I felt we were running okay.

We kept to the right-hand side of the course. Normally a low will go south and then south-east. Clouds had told us it would go straight to the south-east, but not for long, and it would be weak when it did. Then it would go west and would stay in the west – if that's the case you're better off to stay in the west.

We were still racing. The only person who calls a race off is the skipper, and I was not about to do that. As we sailed down towards Tasmania we got the wind in our tail, which made it a little easier to handle the boat. It happened that the course we were sailing was not only one that the boat could handle, it was taking us straight to Tasmania along what sailors call the Tasman Line.

In the morning light helicopters began buzzing

overhead every now and again to see what was going on. We started to get into the lee of Flinders Island, and within radio range of Tasmania. The *Aspect* was okay but other people were not – news the organisers were keeping off the HF. As soon as we tuned in to news bulletins from the land-based radio stations, we realised what was going on.

We understood there had been deaths and which boats were involved, but we still didn't really know .exactly what had happened. We had friends on those boats but who was safe? Who was not? The thing I kept thinking about was that those who had gone had gone. But their loved ones would be full of distress, of the horrible mixture of hope and anguish I knew so well from my father's drowning, as the rescue services kept on searching.

In our 54-foot tub of perspex, aluminium and timber, we were living on the idea that this would finish soon. The weather was telling us that it was going to soften back to 40 or 50 knots, maybe even 30 knots, so we kept shoving more Minties into our pockets and getting on with things.

We knew now, on that second morning, that we were very competitive. It was still blowing quite hard, about 25 or 30 knots out of the south-west, and we were off Flinders, jumping off the top of 20 foot waves with a hollow bang and going as fast as we could. The race was on. 'Let's get this boat up to Constitution Dock real quickly,' I urged the crew. 'Let's just get to the finish line.'

At around 11 o'clock that morning someone managed

to fix the gas. Hot cups of tea and coffee – the best any of us had ever tasted – were passed around, pulling colour back through faces that had turned pale with shock. Travis started chatting away: Did you see this, did you see that? Morale suddenly went through the roof.

Everything had gone mouldy downstairs, including the bread which was now completely green. We figured it could not be that serious, so someone started scraping the mould off the bread to make the crew green sand-wiches. They disappeared quicker than you could say penicillin.

By that afternoon the wind was down to about 20 knots and we were clipping the Tasmanian coast. The cooker was working, some of the instruments were back online and the crew were laughing and joking. They knew now that they had been tested.

The best news was that while the rest of the fleet had cleared out and were 20–30 miles ahead of us, they were also 30–40 miles to leeward. Which effectively meant we had 15 miles on them. Suddenly the team kicked the *Aspect* into overdrive. Halfway down the Tasmanian coast we caught up with a boat called *Midnight Rambler* – a 35-footer that had sailed a fantastic race and beaten us so far. The rest of the fleet was still way out to sea to the left of us as we put up the biggest sails we had on the boat to catch what was left of the wind on flat seas.

We rounded Tasman Light at dusk, watching the lights of Hobart twinkle on the horizon. Tradition dictates that you should be able to come so close to the Tasman Light that you can throw an apple core onto the rock, so Travis dutifully tried to do just that. Beyond us lay Constitution Dock; in a few hours we would be home.

That night we fell through the darkness trying to keep astern of us two yachts that were closing in. We were not sure who they were but they were constantly closing. Damn, they caught up and ran straight past us.

The boat was going well, the crew were going well, and it looked like we might win our handicap. As those thoughts rushed through my exhausted head, I felt myself switch off emotionally.

The sky began lightening in the east, turning the Derwent into a ribbon of silver. Bullets of wind rushed down off Mount Wellington, the 1270-metre peak just west of Hobart. The foredeck team raced to change sails to meet each changing wind condition. The boat was going well, even though she had had the shit kicked out of her.

We were coming off Storm Bay and the boat had taken some major damage. She had crushed panels on the port bow and the port side had some frame delamination. It might sound cosmetic but it is serious; it means there is structural damage to the hull, sections of which were separating from each other because of the massive impact of the waves. My boat was coming apart. We had a lot of running damage, the sea waves had pushed in steel railings and things were battered and bruised downstairs. I was feeling for my boat and tears rolled down my face as we approached the end of the race. The *Aspect* lifted her bow, brought her head to weather, and lunged over the line at 4 am on the morning of December 29.

A runabout chugged alongside. 'Congratulations,' came the call. 'You are ninth in overall, and first to cross the line in your division. You have won.'

I heard the words but echoing around in my head were some verses from a poem that Dad used to read to me when I was a child, at night. It was 'The Man from Snowy River' and in some of the final lines, Banjo Paterson could for all the world have been talking about our poor, battered boat and what we had just been through:

> . . . *his hardy mountain pony he could scarcely raise a trot,*
> *He was blood from hip to shoulder from the spur;*
> *But his pluck was still undaunted, and his courage fiery hot,*
> *For never yet was mountain horse a cur.*

As the tears rolled down my cheeks I thought about my father, and the water; about the other people who had lost their lives over the past few days.

'You all worked incredibly well to get us here. I am so proud of you,' I heard myself telling the crew, over and over again. 'So very, very proud.'

Someone from the CYC jumped on board. 'Have you got any family you can ring? You should let them know you are okay.' Sandy, who would have nightmares about being trapped underwater for weeks after she had got off the boat, was resistant. 'I'll wait,' she tried to say. 'It's too early.'

'No,' came the reply. 'You should ring them. Now.'

She called her parents, waking them up. They were ecstatic to know she was alright. Not long afterwards, her son Gareth, who was at Coffs Harbour, rang her on her mobile. When she answered, he broke down because he had been totally unable to find out how she was. He didn't think he had a mother any more.

The press met us at the dock, with what felt like thousands of TV cameras, microphones, questions and confusion lighting up the freezing, pre-dawn cold. I could barely see where the marina walkway was because of the camera lights in my eyes.

Travis's mother pushed her way through the crowd and grabbed hold of her son to make sure he was alive and real. She held him so tightly it seemed that she would never let him go again. For much of the race she, too, had had no idea whether he was alive or dead. She had phoned the helplines, unable to get through, then begged the CYC for information.

'How are you?' she sobbed as the skinny boy disappeared inside her endless hug. 'Are you alright? Tell me you are alright.'

Suddenly we were all being interviewed and frankly I didn't give a shit. I did not want to talk to the media. All I wanted to do was walk through the reporters, get out of my totally disgusting wet weather gear, march into the nearest dining room and order breakfast. We had made it. Other sailors had not, and all the while the world had been watching. What on earth could we say?

Some of us knew those who had died – John Dean, Jim Lawler and Mike Bannister (all from the *Winston Churchill*), Phil Skeggs and Bruce Guy (from the *Business Post Naiad*) and Glyn Charles (*Sword of Orion*). We were over the moon because of what we had achieved, and rightly so. But our emotions were tempered by guilt for feeling like that because so many wives, brothers, sisters, friends and children were suffering. Death walks alongside us every moment of our life, we all know that. Yet when it comes, you are elated that it wasn't you who was taken that day.

The aftermath lasted far longer than the beautiful white wreaths, each containing a single rose for each sailor who had perished, that lay floating in the dock at Hobart. Some stories have never come out about that race, and never will, even at the inquiry that followed, where blame was apportioned and recommendations weighed.

The rules changed after the '98 Sydney to Hobart. The kind of safety equipment we used became mandatory on all boats, as did the need to have crew members who had completed sea survival courses and parade boats with their storm sails up before any long race. Children under eighteen, such as Travis, were banned.

We did not find ourselves talking too much about those who turned back early. We didn't give them any accolades. And yet they probably displayed the most skill and judgment of anybody on the fleet. They saved themselves and did not put the people in the rescue helicopters at risk. They were heroes, to my mind.

That's not to say the call to continue racing was a bad one. Outside the sport, some started saying yacht racing was too dangerous to continue. Well, they are right. Ocean yacht racers might get their fingers chopped off. They might break arms, crack ribs, scare themselves shitless. They might even die. All those things come at a cost to our society. But what is the cost of not doing things? To ban anything dangerous is to deny being human and, frankly, I don't want to play that game. I want to live in a world where we push the edges. I want to feel the pain and try to survive. I would rather die than live a life where those things are denied me. Because that is not living, in my book.

12

THE CARPE DIEM HAD GONE as far as she could go. She had served us well and I would like to think she was in as good shape after being repaired as the day I finished building her, but Sailors with disAbilities had moved on. What we needed now was a pure-bred racing boat that would not only go faster but carry many more disabled people on board. The cockpit of the *Carpe Diem* could only hold one wheelchair and that was not good enough. If we were going to do more work with children, we needed much more space in the back.

I hemmed and hawed about it for some time, and talked the problem over with David Lyons, the man who was going to design the new boat. The big issue was money. My dream was a million-dollar racer, but we had nowhere near that much to spend. Selling the old boat would raise a fair chunk of the budget needed, and

I could put some more of my own money into it, but sponsorship was going to be critical.

I had a chat to Aspect Computing's Pete Draney, who agreed to help both via his company and personally, yet again. The fibreglass supply company FGI also came to the party. So in July 1999, I sold the *Carpe Diem* to a buyer in Adelaide. We started building the new boat on November 1, and we were working to deadline – it had to be ready for the Sydney to Southport yacht race on June 1. Seven months. No problem for a multi-million-dollar professional racing outfit who could throw all the money in the world at the project. Not so easy for a cash-strapped organisation like us. How the hell were we going to do it?

We got the specifications down. The boat would be a 9-tonne, 10-berth, 16.2 metre racing snake. It would have a 25.8 metre mast, a 48 horsepower engine and a maximum sailing speed of 25 knots. It would need everything from a deep, long trench at the companionway exit for easy access on and off, to a specially set grinder for wheelchair winch operators. Inside, things would be pared down to the bone. My skipper's cabin bit the dust, as did the freezer, fridge and hot water systems. This boat was not being designed for cruising comfort. It was meant to go fast.

The skills I had honed over the years in business came back into the fore as I harangued people, in the nicest way possible, to help us out. It was not so much scavenging as making deals. Going to someone and saying, 'Look, mate, I know this is what you normally charge; I can't afford to pay it. What can I do to help you so you can help me out here? How can we put this together?'

I did favours for everybody all over the place. If someone was a member of the Rotary Club and told me 'Okay, I will do this for you if you do two talks at the club' then hell, I was happy to do that. I love telling people about what we are doing anyway. Others chipped in and surprised us. The president of a nearby Lions Club got a donation together and bought us a spinnaker, which we are using to this day. The local toolmaker did a lot of machine work for us and refused to charge the full price. A foundry in Bankstown bought the entire keel for us after I explained what we were doing.

I sold off bits I had kept from the old *Carpe Diem* to fund the new boat, getting around $8000 for the aluminium mast – a drop in the ocean compared to the $120,000 carbon fibre beauty we wanted set in the heart of the new boat. There were other headaches. The craning costs of building the yacht came in at about $15,000 – lifting it up, putting it down, moving it, taking the keel off, turning it over, all had money haemorrhaging everywhere.

A friend of mine suggested that the owner of a local crane company might be able to do a deal. I sounded him out. He asked me what we needed, I told him a 50-tonne crane, he had a look at our specifications, and agreed, yes, that was what it was going to take.

'How much is all this going to cost?' I asked.

'We'll sort it out,' he replied.

'No, no, no,' I said. 'We are on a really limited budget and I might not be able to afford it. Tell me.'

'Look, mate, let's not discuss this now. What I will tell you is that it will be alright.'

We shook hands and went ahead. Finally the great day arrived. The new boat was done, sitting there in its cradle. I went up to him and said, 'What do we owe you?'

He shook his head. 'My child has cancer, leukaemia, and she went out on your boat two years ago on Sydney Harbour and had the day of her life. She came back so happy and excited. She wouldn't stop talking about it for days. Really, mate, don't worry about it. This one is on me.'

So the boat was complete. She was sparkling, primed and beautiful. But the cost had been higher than I could ever have imagined. While it was being built I became a man possessed, pushing people within SWD like buggery to get things done. Many were helping out of the goodness of their hearts – SWD runs as a charity, nobody gets paid – and we were horribly behind schedule. We had to have the boat in the water to go on the Sydney to Southport or we would jeopardise the whole of that year's sailing campaign, and I pushed some people over the edge. Crew who were keen to be on the boat stopped turning up because when they did I would be yelling and abusing them. I damaged some friend-ships very seriously and before I knew it I had a mutiny on my hands. They had had enough and I responded with the reaction those who knew me had come to expect: 'Fine. Fuck you. I will do it on my own.' So they all told me to get stuffed and some of them never came back, which is a horrible shame.

Adding irony to insult, we missed the Sydney to Southport race anyway. The boat was built but I didn't feel that everything was quite ready.

Then in the middle of all this I was struck by an idea, what Albert Lee would call 'one of David's crazy schemes'. I turned the notion over in my mind and thought it through. It certainly seemed better than my half-baked plan of circumnavigating Antarctica (too bloody cold – I do not like that kind of weather), or trekking across the Simpson Desert with a bunch of wheelies. That idea would have served SWD's purposes well as a stunt to attract attention to the disabled; it would be newsworthy enough to keep our sponsors happy and would be a tremendous achievement for those involved.

'Wheels in the Desert', as I called it in my head, bit the dry red dust. The idea was too far from the heart of what we did: sailing. This latest thought, though, had potential, on every front. It was not just a stunt, it was about our crew breaking a record and becoming so newsworthy that people all over Australia, all over the world, would say, 'Far out, look what the disabled can do.' It would make children believe that they can be bigger than society tells them they are going to be. But could we really do it? Yes, I thought to myself, we could.

I put it aside for the moment, and had my mother christen the new boat *Kayle*, which is a combination of my daughters' names, Gayle and Katie. The gesture felt right. While the boat-building was tearing us all to pieces, my daughter Katie was having birth pains of her own, and on September 8, 1999 Brittany, my first grand-child, came into our family. The irony is that she might be dyslexic, as might her sister Hannah, who would be born almost exactly three years later. Both of my daughters could be carrying dyslexia in their genes, and either of my granddaughters might inherit the condition that has dominated my life.

Brittany's arrival turned my mother into a great-grandmother and brought home to me just how long Rex, my 78-year-old stepfather, had been in our lives. Eighteen years earlier, at Rex's sixtieth birthday I had agreed to give a speech in his honour in front of all his friends. It set me thinking about who and what he really was, and for the first time I looked at Rex and saw him as a person rather than the enemy. My father was brave; he jumped in a river to save his own son. Well, Rex was brave too. He was always there for Mum.

I recalled driving home to their farm one day after we had been out together buying a tractor. I said, 'I'm tired of calling you Mr Booth. How about I call you Rex?'

'Oh yes,' he said. 'Yes.'

I was in my twenties then. I am in my fifties now, and I do not call him Rex any more. I call him Pa. And I love him.

We berthed the *Kayle* at the CYC in Rushcutters Bay and in between training runs we got on with our Youth Program, holding as many kids' sailing days as we could for everyone from adolescents with kidney failure to deaf, dumb and blind kids. The days we took carers out became a particular favourite. They need some extra support too.

The years developed a routine, swinging around the annual fixtures on the racing programs, the kids' days, and weekend and twilight races on Sydney Harbour, designed for anybody who wants to come on board to see whether they would like to take things further.

I was lucky, my financial situation meant that I could devote all my time to the cause – but that turned into something of a double-edged sword. Racing, kids' days and training – and I sometimes think we have worked with every disabled sailor there is in Australia – is a 100 per cent effort, all the time. The only let-up is when I disappear to my Mum's farm and turn the phone off.

I sometimes feel wedded to this boat. I have floated in and out of relationships, often with people generous enough to help out with the organisation, but nothing has stuck. Maybe I am too demanding. My job, and the job of the people around me, is to let those with disabilities – particularly children – know that their world can be as big as they want it to be. That their potential is limited only by their imagination.

As time went on, more people became involved with the organisation, wanting to push this message. One addition was Phil Thompson, who came on board in 2001. Phil, known as Bear to his mates, is a very experienced sailor and former CYC race director, whose Sydney–Hobart race history includes two line-honour wins.

Bear has fought cancer on and off since the early seventies; he's a left-hander whose entire left arm became so bloated with the disease he had to have it amputated. The night before the operation, he got his swollen arm tattooed with a huge square-rigged sailing ship. That was on October 9, 1990. He sailed the Sydney to Hobart six weeks later.

Bear's behind-the-scenes work for SWD has involved everything from training to crewing on the Youth Program. He also wrote a manual detailing *Kayle* and its procedures, packed with suggestions about how to deal with the different disabilities that come on board. Autistic kids, for example, do not like bright flashing lights, so anyone hoisting sails should avoid doing it in a way that might cause the sunlight to bounce around and disturb them.

We sporadically saw children with dyslexia and the more tales I heard, the more angry I became. That any of these children were undergoing what I considered to be abuse at the hands of their schools infuriated me, as does the fact that, unlike in the US or the UK, state schools refuse to label children with dyslexia. One argument is that it would stigmatise them. What it means in practice is that the condition sometimes goes undiagnosed and untreated – even parents with cash behind them can have a huge struggle to get acknowledgment and decent treatment. It's ridiculous. If you don't name something, how can you deal with it? Mention the term Department of Education to me, and I will let you know exactly what I think of that organisation. They allowed my schools to teach me that I was an idiot, and the same thing is going on today. They have a lot to answer for, and they should be brought to account.

I look back on my life and thank my stars that I have

had the ocean. I was one of the lucky ones. There are links between illiteracy, dyslexia and suicide – just as there are links between illiteracy, dyslexia and crime – and the fact that children are going through what I endured almost fifty years ago staggers me. The beatings may have stopped but the humiliations continue. It has taken legal action to change the law in other countries, dragging individual teachers through the courts on duty of care issues. If it takes that to shake things up here, then I will do it. All I can say to those doing the wrong thing is Watch This Space.

I am not alone. In late 2002, a literacy expert told a conference in Sydney that almost one in five adults in this country has such low reading skills that they cannot cope with everyday tasks such as filling in forms or working out exactly how much medicine they should be giving their child from the information printed on the packaging.

For me, it is too late, even though I sometimes get several calls a week from jokers trying to tell me they can cure me. My memory for whole words has increased over the years, but I will never be able to read as most people understand it. Even young Travis Foley will probably never manage it. He left school at fifteen. He lives in a New South Wales country town where youth unemployment is rife. He got himself a job, kept that job, bought himself a boat, built a workshop and is now planning to teach himself wood-turning in the evenings. I am so proud of him.

On board *Kayle*, adult sailors kept coming and going, sporting every kind of disability under the sun. Some were born with their disabilities. Others had had mishaps in childhood and had taken years to overcome them. A third group became disabled as adults – a crystallised version of what humanity is all about. Having accidents is a little like drunkenness in that people become extreme versions of themselves and no one really knows which way they will go until it happens to them. You see the absolute best and the absolute worst.

Some will pull you to one side and tell you how to rort the benefit system. Others will come on board taking so little care of the 'criminal' part of their body – such as a suddenly useless pair of legs – that they will allow sores to fester that could result in needless amputations. And then there are the Vinny Lauwers of this world, who refuse point-blank to let anything get in their way.

I still do not think Vinny has received anywhere near the recognition that he should have done for becoming the first disabled person to sail solo around the world. In my mind that rates as one of the great feats ever, right up there with Hillary and Everest. It is hard enough climbing to the top of a mast in a fully crewed boat. Try climbing to the top of a mast, on your own, in the middle of the huge waves of the Southern Ocean, dragging a useless pair of legs behind you. Ninety-nine per cent of us would have bailed out. Not Vinny. I found myself saying just that to an audience at one of an increasing number of speaking events I had started doing: that whether you are born with disabilities or have them thrust upon you, you should always remember that disability is a state of mind, not a physical condition. I can sail better than most people I know. Does that make them disabled? You tell me.

I remain a grumpy old bastard who should probably keep his temper in check more than he does. You ain't going to make an omelette without breaking eggs, and I have broken a lot over the years. I make mistakes and there is a huge list of people I have offended. Some say I'm hard. Do you do what we have done if you are nice? I don't think so. My purpose in life is to change attitudes about the disabled and I am cranky, and annoying, and I am bloody-well going to reach my goals.

There needs to be a revolution, which is exactly what my crazy scheme was all about. It took me ages to float it with the others but eventually I outlined it at a meeting with some friends, including Phil Thompson and SWD publicist Melinda Lyons. We would sail around Australia – over 6500 nautical miles – nonstop, without coming into port, with an entirely disabled crew, and we would break the Australian circumnavigation record into the bargain.

My best information was that Kanga Birtles held the record of 43 days, 19 hours, 29 minutes and 55 seconds, which he set sailing the *Magna Data* in 1999. In July 2002, the catamaran *Raw Nerve* took the record on but had to pull out after a few days when their rig collapsed. Equipment failure aside, I saw no reason why we could not smash that record. We would have to take everything we needed on board – as soon as we came in to port it would all be over. A water-maker designed to turn salt water into fresh drinking water would deal with our hydration needs.

Our best bet would be to leave roughly between mid-to late May when the conditions were on our side. Travelling north from Sydney, the winds would be blowing basically the right way on every leg of our trip at that time of year – downhill, fast. The toughest stretch would probably be deep in the Southern Ocean where we would have to go down to about 45 degrees south to skirt around the bottom of Tasmania. There can be very big waves there, and it is cold in mid-winter. Cold and yukky.

The scheme had a beautiful symmetry to it: an Australian bunch of weirdos, sailing around Australia, in a boat owned by Australians, sponsored by Australian companies. Disabled people competing with the able-bodied on their own terms. A revolution, in both senses of the word. What I did not tell my SWD mates was that this was to be a precursor to a much bigger plan that would take several more years to hatch. I will need a lot of money for the next one, and it will be worth every dollar.

Melinda thought Around Australia was a terrific idea, perfect for SWD's publicity needs, and began thinking about how to maximise it: constant email contact with the crew, weblink updates daily to the SWD website, and filming, which would be beamed via satellite to (hopefully) a TV channel interested in charting *Kayle*'s record-breaking progress. Phil, too, thought it had legs. Ever the level-headed one, he was aware there were going to be difficulties. Money was not one of them: I talked to Pete Draney about funding and, yet again, he said yes.

The toughest thing would probably be the personalities. The people I wanted on board are all very strong-
minded individuals who had refused to let their
disabilities get in their way, in life or in racing. When a
big gale comes and blows its head off, they would all
just get to work. It was the racing lulls that would be
the problem. If you have no common enemy, what
happens when suddenly the sailor next to you, who has
not had a bath in twenty days, starts stirring his coffee
the wrong way?

I made a mental list of who I wanted on board and
approached them one by one. I telephoned Kim Jaggar,
the principal of Sydney Boys High School, who had lost
most of his left arm in a skiing accident at Thredbo when
he was twelve. Kim had gone straight back to skiing
after his accident, with his competitive racing ambitions
shattered. He was a tremendously experienced racing
sailor when he did the first Hobart with SWD in 1995
and has been with the old 'Cripple Express', as he calls
our boat, ever since, watching the changes in those angry
and depressed about the misfortunes that have befallen
them. 'This sort of activity involves teamwork, other
people and being prepared to help out,' he tells those
who ask about yachting and the disabled. 'The key to it
all is a test of character . . . What you are made of, that
is what you find out when you go ocean racing.'

Kim agreed to join Around Australia. Great. Part of
the appeal for him was Matthew Flinders' historic map-
ping of the continent: we would be going west-about,
as Flinders did. There was another thing. 'It will be nice

to take a bit of a break from the extremely demanding situation I find myself in.' A holiday, then? He thinks so. 'I imagine it is going to be much easier than what I'm doing now.'

Double amputee Albert Lee also jumped at the chance. Polio victim Al Grundy said it sounded like fun to him and, anyway, he was sick of doing Sydney to Hobarts. Harald Mirlieb's first response was that he would have to check with his wife, Terje. She was keener for him to do that than yet another Hobart, which takes up so much of Harald's time over the Christmas break. Harald, who is deaf, gets bored with things pretty easily; he, too, was after another challenge.

Brett Pearce was the baby of the bunch. Born in 1976 with spina bifida, Brett has limited strength but full use of his arms and legs. He is another who thrives on challenges – 'They didn't think I would walk when I was born; I proved them wrong.' He only began sailing in February 2001, after kidney damage forced a lifestyle change. Around the same time he saw the SWD Sydney to Hobart documentary that was made back in 1994. Brett barely waited until I had finished explaining the plan to say yes. He loves sailing, and the freedom it offers, telling people that his condition doesn't matter so much when he is on a boat. His main worry was the grinding impact of spending so much time in a confined space with so many other people.

Phil Thompson's concerns were more serious. After a long history of fighting cancer, Bear is dying. He is suffering severely from the side effects of years of treatment.

His heart functions at a third of the rate it should, and he rejected the idea of a transplant because it would ultimately mean he would not be able to sail. His main worry about the trip was simple: 'That I will not survive it. The obvious problems are jeopardising the entire event and just the strain on the others. But having said that, we all need to be very aware of one another's limitations. The mental side of things is going to make or break this trip.'

So why is he going to do it? 'It is just the way I am. I do the things that I can to challenge myself. Otherwise you just curl up and stay in bed. By setting goals you are challenging the boundaries . . . I don't necessarily always achieve those goals but I have got to give it a go. It's my way of survival.'

This book began with me but it belongs to all disabled people and everyone who has ever cared for them. I am older now, and I see young blokes on the boat doing things, without thinking twice, that I can no longer manage. In my prime I could outswim and outsail any of them, but they are the ones walking down the road without a care in the world and I sometimes feel as though I am falling apart.

But I am closer now than I ever have been to the woolly-headed child who ran off to primary school fifty-odd years ago so full of hope and happiness. That boy understands exactly why we are waiting for our perfect winter day to appear. He knows that we will recognise it because the wind will blow hard from the south and the currents will beckon.

And when that day comes, I will do exactly what I have done all my life, man and boy. I will run out of the house, grabbing whatever I need on the way, and I will disappear.

On to the water.

Acknowledgements

I want to thank my daughters, Gayle and Katie, my sister Bronnie and the rest of my family, including my grandparents, Alan Booth, Robyn Booth, Paul Booth, Harry Pescud, George Pescud, Josie Barber and Aunt Betty, who was always there for me when it really mattered. Enormous thanks to Pete Draney, whose support for Sailors with disAbilities has been extraordinary from the very start; also to Sharon Bond, Cathy Josling and everybody who has helped with the organisation, past and present. I wish I could list every single one of your names here but there simply is not room. Thanks also to my dear friend Alan Cooper; to Don Jeffries, Don McNeice, Alex Hutt, Ross Griffiths, Margaret Stuart and Elizabeth Beards.

To all whose names I have spelt wrong, what can I say? I'm dyslexic, for Christ's sake.

David Pescud, February 2003